STRANGE SKIES, STRANGE EYES
The Paranormal, Ufology and Everyday Magick

Brian Allan

Typeset by Jonathan Downes, Andrea Rider
Cover and Layout by SPiderKaT for CFZ Communications
Using Microsoft Word 2000, Microsoft Publisher 2000, Adobe Photoshop CS.

First published in Great Britain by CFZ Press

CFZ Press
Myrtle Cottage
Woolsery
Bideford
North Devon
EX39 5QR

© CFZ MMXV

ISBN: 978-1-909488-24-3

Foreword
by Brad and Sherry Steiger

E ven those readers who have an open mind concerning the vagaries of the reports and the variety of theories regarding the UFO enigma might find it a bit disconcerting to approach a book entitled Strange Skies, Strange Eyes and subtitled, The Paranormal, Ufology, and Everyday Magick. For many students and investigators of the Great Mystery of the unidentified objects in our skies, it is decidedly heretical to mention what they deem as extraterrestrial visitors to our planet in the same sentence as the paranormal. And then to include the subject of Magick in the mix, why that is akin to madness and, in an earlier age, would be burning at the stake for heresy.

We may exaggerate the penalties of UFO orthodoxy concerning those who dare to mix the strangers in our skies with the paranormal and its poltergeists thumping in the night plus the folklore of the occult, but the UFO purist who has believed for so long that "they," the extraterrestrials, walk among us, even breed hybrids among us, will find the combination decidedly off-putting. And perhaps such a blend of mysteries could be an incredulous stretch of mind and imagination if Strange Skies, Strange Eyes were not written by such a scholar and meticulous researcher as Brian Allan.

The care with which Allan has written this book is a testament to his years of study and his decades of proven prowess as a careful journalist of the three areas of exploration that he has chosen for this remarkable book—UFOs, the paranormal, and the undeniable, often unconscious, practice of Magick and organized religion. Allan's style combines superb scholarship with an easy-to-read style that renders concepts that might be difficult and obscure in a less practiced author's prose. Readers, who confront what at first might seem a formidable topic, effortlessly read through the text and then find themselves agreeing with the author's argument or easily accepting his fresh theory of the strange and the unknown.

Allan begins his unique odyssey of the paranormal and Ufology by examining with fresh insight the mystery of just how far Nazi technology and German mysticism may have combined energies scientific and spiritual to make contact with extraterrestrial intelligence and receive otherworldly counsel regarding both advanced weaponry and futuristic space vehicles. How real were the extraterrestrial contacts provided by the German mystics and mediums and how deep was the Fuhrer's perverted discipleship before the two philosophies and technologies clashed and burned? Allan does not neglect the members of the esoteric and the UFO field who have revealed themselves to be agents of disinformation, and he objectively analyzes the oft-heard accounts of underground alien bases and the disturbing claims of clashes between Earth's invaders and special military forces of its governments.

The author painstakingly examines such accounts and carefully evaluates just how much of such alleged interplanetary war stories we might believe. No paranormal, mystical, magical, supernatural topic remains unexamined by Allan's decision to make this a book with an incredibly wide sweep. The Satanic majesty and his army of demons, nasty buggers, who required practiced exorcisms, are represented. There are a host of monsters, including vampires, who try to conquer the pages of the book. However, just when readers might be growing fearful of the influence of the Darkside, Allan refreshes us with accounts of miracles that soundly force Satan to vacate our rooms and to leave our souls unscathed. This is a book for the reader who wishes a detailed, straightforward, examination of a multitude of paranormal phenomena explained in an unbiased manner, layered with an objective analysis of decades of UFO manifestations, coupled with a dispassionate analysis of the uses and practices of everyday Magick. We highly recommend Strange Skies, Strange Eyes: The Paranormal, Ufology, and Everyday Magick.

Brad and Sherry Steiger, authors of Mysteries of Time and Space and Real Encounters, Different Dimensions, and Otherworldly Beings.

Acknowledgements

I would like to express my thanks to my dear wife who sits with admirable patience and good humour (not to mention offering sage advice and common sense) listening to the continually changing and not necessarily coherent spread of ideas that come tumbling out while I'm writing. I'd also like to express my thanks to Don Philips for his unstinting help and support, and also to his friend Becky, whose absolutely unique insights have also been invaluable: I should add that Becky is a spirit! My thanks also goes to Brad and Sherry Steiger for supplying the forward for this book, my deep appreciation to you both. Another person who deserves mention is the indefatigable Steve Mera, my co-pilot and good friend, with whom I produce the rather splendid and always thought provoking digital publication, Phenomena Magazine. Finally, I'd like to thank the ever-reliable Richard T. Cole for providing the stunning artwork that adorns the cover of this book, more power to his digital brush.

Contents

Part Two
Everyday Magick

Introduction

This book could best be described as a series of reflections and observations, a distillation if you like, on the nature of, and relationship between, the occult as we encounter it in our daily lives. This includes the paranormal in all its guises and how this impinges upon the often fractious subject of Ufology, aspects of which may in themselves be other manifestations of the paranormal. From my own investigations and researches it seems to me that there is little if any difference between any of these subjects and where any divergences do occur, they are almost certainly in how different individuals experience and interpret the individual components.

Some of these differences are cultural and some are social, while others may be produced by various religious beliefs and affiliations. This is before one factors in the sophistication of the era in which they were experienced, because this invariably has a major effect on the interpretation. There is one slight caveat here, because there exists the possibility that the very naivety of the early cultures may actually have allowed them to see the nature of various phenomena for what they really were. Perhaps more technically aware and sophisticated cultures (like our own) have applied their own templates of understanding and acceptability to what they were experiencing and in doing so saw what they expected to see and because of that completely missed the point.

Surprisingly, in a classic example of a condition known as cognitive dissonance, many of those who hold one to particular belief however unlikely it might be, are extremely unwilling or unable to accommodate other interpretations of what they believe to be true. People who display this tendency are able to have two (and sometimes more) completely contradictory aspects of a subject running parallel in their minds, but perhaps that is part of the nature of the human condition and how it instinctively manifests faith. Faith is one of the components, perhaps the main component, in the glue that binds belief together for one cannot exist without the other.

The phrase, 'cognitive dissonance', was created by Leon Festinger for his book 'When Prophecy Fails', which detailed the emotional and psychological fallout of the followers of a UFO cult when they discovered that their sincerely held belief in an impending apocalypse did not occur as predicted. Some, understandably disillusioned abandoned the cult, but others became even more deeply enmeshed in its beliefs, almost certainly drawn in by the need for support from others who shared their views, it is how cults function. One of the chapters in the book looks at this bizarre phenomenon in more detail.

Whether it is belief in a supreme deity, the efficacy of magick, the existence of a 'spirit world', that extraterrestrials regularly visit this planet for whatever reason, or even that science and rationality are the only truths worth espousing, it is why we do what we do. It is why hope still flourishes even in the darkest times, it is often what makes living bearable, for without faith in something there is no hope and without hope we have nothing. Where this manifests most starkly is in the strange (or perhaps bizarre) juxtaposition where dedicated and highly qualified scientists are also committed believers in a creator God and this is an apparent absolute contradiction in terms that they somehow manage to justify to themselves.

To be a scientist means that your discipline is entirely based on proof, known facts and carefully measured variables and any experimental work they carry out is done to strict protocols with known or expected outcomes, science cannot operate under any other rules. Belief in a supreme deity who governs the settings of the universe and all it contains requires unswerving faith and absolute belief in something that is immeasurable, unprovable and unknowable, yet still they manage to rationalise it to themselves.

This is especially true when one looks at it the other way round and considers the case of priests and other members of the clergy who are also scientists, but entered their scientific field *after* attaining their religious vocation. This was certainly the case with the monks in the Middle Ages who were also proto-scientists, the astronomers, astrologers and alchemists who made sense of and developed ancient traditions through observation, experimentation and, finally, proof. It has been speculated that some priest/scientists because of their scientific training come to doubt their religious calling and only remained as priests because there was still an element of doubt that prevented them from denying and renouncing their beliefs, plus of course the added and very real likelihood of being denounced as heretics, tried, tortured and then piously murdered.

Another way of looking at this is how mainstream science in an almost knee-jerk reaction utterly refutes and denies the existence of any and all paranormal phenomena simply because it refuses to comply with or obey its rules: in other words it cannot be defined, predicted or measured: yet still it happens. Perhaps Newtonian science has some practical limitations and although it serves perfectly well in most areas it is useless in others. It is interesting that when Newtonian science, let's call it 'conventional science' and the science of quantum mechanics meet, the union is far from easy, because conventional science still harbours deep suspicions about the validity of quantum science. This is because the science of the vanishingly small is almost unimaginably different from that of the impossibly large. At the subatomic level the impossible becomes possible and disconcertingly, when experiments have been conducted to prove the accuracy of these they have been proved correct *every single time.*

Another branch of science that confounds the conventional is psychology and psychiatry and how those areas of science define the nature of consciousness, something that conventional science still cannot satisfactorily explain. This is perhaps best characterised in a quotation from Stanislav Grof, the eminent Czechoslovakian psychiatrist and pioneer of transpersonal psychology, when he said, *'The study of consciousness that can extend beyond the body is extremely important for the issue of survival, since it is this part of human personality that would be likely to survive death.'*.

Another astonishing and highly relevant observation comes from the Nobel prize winning physicist Professor Brian Josephson who has studied paranormal phenomena for more the three decades, according to Prof Josephson, *"Quantum theory is now being fruitfully combined with theories of information and computation. These developments may lead to an explanation of processes still not understood within conventional science such as telepathy – an area where Britain is at the forefront of research."* Needless to say these remarks are regarded as major heresies by mainstream science and will remain so until finally proven true, which eventually they will.

PART ONE
The Paranormal and Ufology

Chapter One
The Occult, Superscience and
The Third Reich

What follows in the first chapter may be regarded in a number of ways; one suggests that in the dying months of the Second Word War, Nazi scientists may have accidentally stumbled across a truly breathtaking technology involving the precursors of time travel. This was branch of science that was so 'out there' and pseudo-scientific that it was never and perhaps could never be officially recognised, or, on the other hand perhaps was recognised, but because of its enormous implications deliberately destroyed and the details permanently suppressed.

Another is that these same German engineers and scientists did not in fact create this particular technology, but instead developed a type of aircraft that was so revolutionary and far ahead of its time in its concept, that even now it has only been partially replicated. Either that, or there was a possible link between the two technologies that, once again, because of the risks involved was never fully exploited. The confusion may have arisen because of the implications and revolutionary (one might even say heretical) principles behind the technology. It should also be pointed out that this subject will take us into regions that are, perhaps, best left well alone, but such is its continuing fascination that, perhaps unavoidably, like moths to a flame we are irresistibly drawn there.

This area is the still unknown, but much speculated upon, link between some areas of technology and magick. It also seems to indicate that at some levels science and the occult are indistinguishable and particle physics seems to be pointing the way, albeit to an audience that is almost too eager to deny it. Whatever the truth, it is clear that 'something', some form of exotic technology was created in those dark days and in spite of continual official denials and obfuscation the story refuses to go away. In this chapter I offer some possibilities and in the interests of fairness (and perhaps sanity) a more credible and, it has to be said, likely alternative. The reader should be aware that this chapter ends with a look at how fiction can, just perhaps, be made real just by thinking about it, it is certainly plausible enough and it may also be how legends are born.

As if the whole subject of UFOs and Ufology were not already sufficiently confused and mired in various schools of conflicting, bizarre and frequently irreconcilable thought, there are also persistent tales about strange and borderline magickal UFO related technologies attempted at the very end of the Second World War. There were several mystical groups operating in Germany prior to the Nazi hegemony of 1930's and 40's that appear, rightly or wrongly, to be inextricably linked to a dangerous, surreal, shadowy UFO/occult/non-human dimension. These groups, and in particular their esoteric beliefs, attracted the interest of several high ranking members among the Nazi elite and were adapted for use within this organisation and its various ideologies.

This was especially true of projects overseen by the notorious and ultra-elite *Shutzstaffel* (more commonly abbreviated as the *SS*) created by Heinrich Himmler, who was also something of an occultist and heavily influenced by the ideas and theories of Karl Maria Wiligut, Guido Von List and others, albeit where this impinged on Germanic racial and cultural origins. Why this should be is far from clear, although its founder certainly did harbour several quasi-mystical ambitions for his murderous organisation. It is likely that he regarded them as some kind of latter-day version of the Teutonic Knights, an idealised and ultra-loyal praetorian guard of pure Aryan stock.

This is partly demonstrated in the use of double '*sig*' rune forever associated with the *SS*, which was originally connected to a form of sun worship, but its meaning was later altered to mean 'victory'. It is also likely that due to the manner in which the *SS* was financed it could afford to dabble in projects that, because of their implications, might have daunted other organisations. Due to the considerable influence, constant lobbying (and of course malign reputation) of Heinrich Himmler, it is said that the only person in his sphere of influence not afraid of him was Adolph Hitler. Interestingly, unlike Himmler who had an abiding passion for the subject, although Adolph Hitler is because of his magnetic personality often given credit as an occult adept, there is no hard evidence to suggest that this is true.

Much of the information about Hitler's presumed occult connections comes from a very influential work entitled '*The Spear of Destiny*' by Trevor Ravenscroft, which, although undeniably readable and entertaining, may not necessarily be entirely accurate. However, as we shall discover when one becomes involved in this particular subject it all rather depends on how one interprets the available information. To be sure it can easily, perhaps too easily, be viewed in a purely rational manner, but when one allows oneself the luxury of an open mind, as we shall soon see the possibilities are fascinating...and endless. This is especially true when one contemplates the very nature of evil and whether or not it is a discrete force.

Immediately after its final incarnation as the fully fledged *SS* (it began in 1922 as a smaller and much more humble organisation, certainly not the black uniformed ideological bludgeon that smashed its way across the battlefield). To facilitate the way in which it operated it was deliberately funded as a separate entity existing outside the approved German military budget.

Coincidentally, this is exactly how the American CIA is funded, which in effect makes it unaccountable to the US Government and explains why, like the *SS*, it was also able to fund many 'off the wall' projects like the 'Stargate' remote viewing exercise that would normally be refused on a whole host of legal, ethical and/or moral grounds. That said and given its ideology, the inflexible *SS* would not have been affected by anything as mundane as ethics or morality in its genocidal crusades and pogroms. It is arguable that the SS was perhaps the ultimate incarnation of the destructive cult at its very worst.

The notoriety of the *SS* is such that, in recent times at least, they have become the very embodiment and essence of evil as portrayed in video games like the 'Nazi Zombies' add-ons that appear on the consistently excellent 'Call of Duty' series and also in a number of low budget horror films such as the cultish (and rather good) 'Outpost' franchise, although there are several others. It is clear that whoever scripted the Outpost films, which feature a legion of undead *SS* troopers hidden in a rift in the space/time continuum, must have read at least some of the fevered speculation surrounding the jaw dropping technology that the Nazi's may (or equally may not) have been in the process of developing. We will consider this a little later. What is certain is that because of what it was capable of and what it actually did, the *SS* as an organisation has, if anything, become even more iconic, loathed and feared than when it actually existed.

However, what is certain is that by that late stage of the Second World War, the Nazi Party and the scientists and engineers who were still fanatically loyal to its aims would try literally *anything* to snatch victory from the jaws of defeat. This apparently included an attempt at actualising Einstein's Unified Field theory and what that might reveal in terms of creating a super-weapon that might, even in the final months and weeks turn the tide of war in Germany's favour. Examples of other attempts to create new and innovative (albeit conventional) weapons are well attested, with the various armaments being hurried into service with minimal development.

This ordnance ranged from the mundane, like the worlds first assault rifle, the Sturmgewehr 44, through to fledgling cruise missiles like the V1, which eventually led to the V2 rocket, and there were also plans for another generation of missiles. These were the A9 and A10, which would have been the worlds first functional Intercontinental Ballistic Missiles (ICBM's) and were intended to strike at the USA. There were also various types of jet and rocket propelled fighter aircraft in development, and we will also look at some of these in more detail in a later chapter, plus flying-wing bombers, tanks, unusual acoustic and electrical devices and even a species of energy weapon, which was a very early form of laser. Whatever one may think of the Nazi's and their distorted philosophies there is no doubt that, technologically at least, they were extremely talented.

They also attempted to construct an atomic bomb, something they failed to do because. Although it is not generally appreciated, Nazi Germany did have two nuclear reactors and one of them located at Haigerloch near Stuttgart was actually functional, but had not yet been adapted to enrich uranium to weapons grade; and for that we must all be eternally thankful. Genuinely remarkable and innovative as those inventions were, there are also rumours and guarded hints of others, that for variety of reasons (probably time and resources) were never brought to fruition. Of these much speculated upon devices, one lay at the very cutting edge of what might have been technologically possible at the time, this was a circular aircraft capable of vertical take off, remarkable manoeuvrability and an astonishing turn of speed, but, vitally, still fell within the realms of conventional (albeit innovative) engineering, but there may have been another even more astonishing project afoot that did not.

This device was apparently actually built, but is difficult to categorise because it was intended to explore areas of physics perhaps more familiar to sorcerers than scientists and was evidently intended to either defy gravity, punch a hole in the very fabric of space/time or something else that beggars belief. Was this an impossible pipe dream? The answer is no, it was not; or at least not necessarily, for it is only now as our knowledge of what lies within the realm of the quantum physics increases that we begin to understand what these scientific pioneers just might have attempted.

While it is arguable that what the Nazi scientists found was only a by-product of their quest to perfect something else, i.e. a type of aircraft, further investigation indicates that the results obtained using the device may, unlikely as it might appear, have been its intended function all along. Perhaps the aircraft was a ruse employed in the manner that some intelligence and military agencies still use Ufology as a cover for the own nefarious 'black projects. It seems that very little is new and intelligence services, irrespective of the country, have always operated in near identical ways.

As regards this particular possibility, we should look at some of those attempting to create a weapon capable of giving Nazi Germany a last throw of the dice to stave of what was increasingly becoming certain defeat. Many of those involved had good reason to do so, because the fear of possible retribution must have weighed heavily on their minds...if not consciences. It is known that towards the end of the war, along with such notables as Werner von Braun and a high ranking artillery officer, Major General Walter Dornberger, plus the enigmatic and capable *SS* general Hans Kammler became involved in developing the V2 rocket and its many variants.

The difference is that Hans Kammler was in a unique position because he was tasked with the supervision of various, extremely exotic 'special projects' that were right outside the remit of other scientists and specialists. This would have been quite possible because the *SS* was highly compartmentalised in matters of security, so that people and groups only knew what they absolutely needed to and those involved with these aptly named 'special projects' would have been isolated from the other groups. The fearsome reputation of the *SS* ensured that idle curiosity or speculation was not an option.

Due to their abilities and technological know-how many of them were eventually swept up by the enormous 'technology grab' of the USA's Operation Paperclip (so-called because paperclips were used to mark the files of scientists considered to be of particular interest to the Americans). It was no accident that scientists and engineers like Werner von Braun eventually went on to carve a niche in the US missile programme, helped create NASA and supervised the Apollo moon project, while Dornberger became a vice-president of the Bell Aircraft Company. However Kammler's fate is much less clear because next to nothing is known about what finally became of him. It has been suggested that he was killed either by the Russians or perhaps the Czech resistance while attempting to flee, but given his vital technological abilities and knowledge it is possible that he too was embraced under the auspices of Operation Paperclip, but nothing was ever said about it. Admittedly that is unlikely, but given the nature of what he was working on nevertheless it cannot be ruled out. There is, however, another near incredible possibility that we shall consider shortly.

Operation Paperclip

Perhaps we should pause briefly to look at Operation Paperclip, because its relevance cannot be overstated and we shall encounter it many times in various roles. Make no mistake about it; rocket and missile technology was not the only aspect of warfare sought by the American and of course other governments. As well as the technologies involved in the V1 and V2, the allied powers were interested in anything that might gave them an edge in the new world order that had emerged from the chaos and inferno of total war. This included a whole variety of specialisations including nuclear energy (for obvious reasons all of the emerging powers had a very keen interest in atomic weapons), communications, electronics, and the queasy techniques of torture, interrogation techniques and 'behavioural modification', i.e. mind control. Various concentration camps like the one at Auschwitz had, amongst other things, been used to test the effectiveness of hypnotics and hallucinogens like Mescaline etc.

Because of this, the expertise unearthed by Paperclip saw the start of such research programmes as Project Chatter (a US navy project designed to evaluate various drugs for use in interrogations), which was based on the research conducted in the concentration camps. Some of the doctors involved ended up at Randolph AFB in Texas to continue their experiments on psychiatric patients and, as with the shameful and wholly unethical Tuskegee Experiment, ethnic minorities There was also the now toxic and discredited CIA mind control programme, MKULTRA; a project that took the work of Project Chatter to the next level and beyond. The experiment was officially disbanded in 1963 and the majority of the really sensitive information shredded in 1973 on the orders of the then CIA director Richard Helm, although it is more than likely that the techniques learned while it was in operation (it started in 1953) still continue with improvements and modifications to this day.

Deny it as they might, all governments have a vested interest in projects such as these and the USA was no more or less guilty than any of the rest, but they were unlucky enough to have been caught at it. The majority of what is known about MKULTRA came to light in the late 1970's and is based on the few files that were missed so the details are sketchy at best, but present a worrying glimpse into a deeply flawed and amoral section of government. It has to be said that for decades, almost since its creation, the CIA had little input other that generous funding from the US government and for many years was virtually autonomous and responsible for several extremely unpleasant projects and operations.

In fact the end of the Second World War saw various countries try to benefit from those who created the innovative weapons technology that was spawned in Germany, with the Russians and Americans in particular trying to outdo one another in just who or what they could appropriate. It is also true that those who devised these weapons realised that their knowledge gave them a strong position from which to negotiate and they used to their advantage. From the German point of view, for very obvious reasons it was getter to go with the Americans than the Russians, who had many bitter and deeply held scores to settle. It does make one wonder about just how their former opponents in the USA and elsewhere managed to rationalise what some of these Nazi scientists actually did and were preparing to do, but I suppose that the quest for new knowledge and with it power must have salved many consciences.

Beyond Paperclip

The results of this sanctioned 'body snatching' eventually became obvious through the way in which both of these superpowers rapidly developed their offensive and defensive technologies. However there was still something missing; any traces of a highly specialised 'super-weapon' called *'Die Glocke'* or *'The Bell'* which reputedly had near magickal properties that lay at the core of Kammler's special projects group. What 'The Bell' was supposedly able to create, along with the alleged 'flying discs', is the basis of a series of long-lasting tales and rumours that just refuse to lie down and although I have some deep personal reservations about the validity of certain information associated with them, on balance I feel that they are worth examining for the following reasons.

Over several decades I have consistently heard and read fragments of information from many diverse and apparently unconnected sources concerning a 'great secret' which was allegedly in the possession of Nazi Germany both during, and especially immediately prior to, the end of Second World War.

Part of the so-called 'great secret' related to a crashed UFO supposedly discovered at Freiburg in the Black Forest during 1936. As with what supposedly occurred years later in 1947 in Roswell, New Mexico, there have been suggestions that this machine was back-engineered, i.e. the technology it contained was examined, evaluated and where possible replicated. However, where the accounts diverge quite markedly is in the involvement of two German mystical and occult organisations, *The Thule Society* and *The Vril Society* in the process.

The input from these groups in the aftermath of the alleged Black Forest UFO retrieval was apparently vital, because this could not have been a straightforward back-engineering project, simply because, as is likely, some of the technology involved would have obeyed no scientific principles known at the time. This problem was supposedly overcome when the practical knowledge obtained from the craft was combined with information channelled by the Vril Society and the captured spaceship rendered capable of flight. On the other hand, what was involved with 'The Bell' was based entirely on technology, although admittedly at the very ragged edge of what was (or might be) possible, and is something quite different, because it abuts areas of specialisation and knowledge where Newtonian scientists are far from comfortable.

These rumours have been consistent and widespread, which leads me to the conclusion that there may be an element of truth in them. That said, it may also be an example of disinformation, where a crumb of truth is mixed in with a vast amount of deception and lies. However, it does seem to gel with the bizarre overlay of mysticism and technology that colours much of the information surrounding the subject. In fact it resonates strongly with the famous saying attributed to the late Arthur C Clarke, *'Any sufficiently advanced technology is indistinguishable from magick'*, and the more one studies the subject it appears as if he was quite correct. Any technology is genuinely magickal depending on the culture and era that encounters it, which is something that modern scientists and their particle accelerators etc still find almost impossible to accept.

In order to explain these theories, it is first necessary to know a little of some of the occult beliefs prevalent in Europe, especially Germany, in the early part of the 20th century.

The Societies

In the late 1800's, early 1900's there were a variety of secret/occult societies operating in Germany, the main ones were 'The Bavarian Illuminati,' 'The Freemasons,' 'The Rosicrucians,' The Thule Society' and 'The Vril Society'. Each of these five societies, although all based in mysticism and secrecy, had a unique role and function, some even served as nurseries for the ultra-nationalism of the fledgling Nazi Party. Of these five, two were especially noted for their occult connections; The Vril Society and its purely German offshoot The Thule Society. The chief architect of the Thule Society was Baron Rudolph von Sebottendorff, sometimes and more correctly referred to as Rudolf Glauer. Sebottendorff/ Glauer possessed a wide ranging knowledge of mysticism especially the Islamic variety, which encompassed the Dervish sects and particularly the practice of Sufism, which differs markedly from mainstream Islamic teaching.

Thule

The name Thule refers to the capital of the legendary Aryan polar country Hyperborea. Also referred to as *'Ultima Thule'*, it was supposedly the gateway to another world. Thule was therefore recognised as a place where humans could, by whatever means, *'leave the earth'*; it also reputedly stood at a portal leading to the 'Hollow Earth'. Interestingly, the major players in the 20th century, the USA and the Russian Federation have ELF (extra low frequency) transmitters sited in this area. These transmitters are supposedly used to communicate with submarines whilst still submerged, but worryingly they broadcast these signals at brain-wave frequencies of around 18 to 20Hz. This has led to speculation that they are used for another more sinister purpose, a deliberate attempt to influence the thoughts and actions of human beings. If true this is a prime example of modern science performing what would once have been defined as magick.

Traditionally, the Hyperboreans were in contact with extraterrestrials or at least alien cultures in that they were not of this earth, in some versions of this account there was alleged interbreeding. In common with the legendary inhabitants of Atlantis, they engaged in war with neighbouring civilisations. This escalated into the use of atomic weapons, resulting in a Pyrrhic victory for the Hyperboreans, who as well as defeating their enemies, virtually

25

destroyed themselves in the process. In common with genetic radiation damage in recent times, the surviving Hyperboreans were soon faced with the prospect of mutated and otherwise damaged offspring.

Showing remarkable resolve and strong comparison with policies adopted by the Nazis, those that had not sustained any apparent genetic damage banded together and effectively removed themselves from the gene pool in a variety of self imposed quarantine and any 'damaged' offspring from this group were neutered. This early example of practical eugenics was practised until they were sure that any defective genes had been bred out. The other mutated group eventually died out, whether they were 'assisted' in this is open to debate. This may seem like and indeed is a harsh clinical line to adopt, but being faced with the stark choice of the extinction of their entire race, they had little option. In fact although currently vilified and the Nazi's condemned for it, eugenics have been used both officially and otherwise over the years in various countries including the United Kingdom, the USA, Australia, Japan, Russia, China and surprisingly, given how the Jews were treated in Germany, Israel.

The descendants of this seminal 'Mother race' were the Celts, who, like the ripples on a pond, spread out, colonising various northern areas of the planet. Scots, Irish, Basques, Spanish, Scandinavians, Icelanders and the Portuguese, all these peoples are of Celtic origin. These disparate nationalities have one common genetic trait, a large percentage of Rh-negative blood types, which, according to the beliefs of the Thule society, was a characteristic of the Hyperboreans and their extraterrestrial associates. In recent times, the majority of alleged alien abductees are reportedly from RH negative blood groups. Some UFO investigators have indicated that this is a possible indication that ET cultures are tracking their cross-bred progeny; it would certainly make sense. Other races and peoples who posses a positive blood types were considered to be racially impure, as positive blood is thought to be contaminated by contact with the primate evolved strand of human DNA.

Vril

The name 'Vril' is, according to which version of the story you hear, either the Atlantean language, which, atypically, was composed of sounds and clicks, quite unique and similar in form to the communication used by dolphins, or that Vril describes a type of esoteric energy. The word, Vril, is said to come from the ancient Sumerian word *Vri-Il* or 'like God'. The Vril Society itself was founded in the city of Vienna in 1917 by a group of four people, one of whom was the medium Maria Orsic who claimed to be channelling information, which included the 'Magical, violet, black stone', and the Spear of Destiny, directly from extraterrestrials. The source of Vril power was the Black Sun, which is described as being 'an invisible beam of infinite light'. The Black Sun itself was a secret school of philosophical thought thousands of years old and allegedly the foundation upon which the occult beliefs of the Nazi Third Reich were based. *SS* founder Heinrich Himmler was said to be an adept of this ancient doctrine.

Himmler and the Occult

Such was the strength of belief in the occult and its potential power, that Heinrich Himmler, a former Roman Catholic, ordered the construction of a spiritual Valhalla deep below his *SS* fortress at Wewelsberg in Westphalia. He purchased this former ruin in 1934 and had it rebuilt over a number of years at a cost of some 13 million Marks siphoned from the blank cheque that formed the *SS* budget. It was dedicated to the cult and belief system of the *SS*, the Teutonic Knights and other mystical/occult doctrines. Below the castle's elaborate main banqueting hall he ordered the construction of a symbolic *'Hall of the Dead'*, supposedly to house urns containing the ashes and crests of his twelve closest 'disciples' when they died.

This consisted of a circular chamber with twelve low stone platforms around its walls. In the centre of the room, in a circular depression accessed by three steps, was a form of altar. This altar or dais was the focal point of the room. Another school of thought asserts that any attempts to invoke whatever dark, latent mystical powers within the 'Black Sun' would be carried out here. Twelve initiates would stand, one on each of the stone platforms against the walls, facing the central dais. Each one concentrating, summoning up part of the necessary energy, focusing and channelling the power to the celebrant, the high priest, perhaps Himmler in person or an appointee. Certain of these ceremonies allegedly required human blood sacrifice, which presented no difficulty, the concentration camps and prisons were full of them. A small group of victims was reportedly kept at the fortress for this purpose. Given his supposedly fastidious personal habits it is unlikely that Himmler would have been directly involved in any sacrifice, no doubt delegating this duty to a subordinate.

There is no evidence that any dark powers were actually released during these Hellish rituals or even if they were carried out, but depending on your religious persuasion and how one views the conduct of the war, perhaps they were. One thing is certain, if they were not it wasn't for the lack of trying. The emblem of the 'Black Sun' was essentially an elaborate mandala, like a spoked wheel surrounded by runic symbols. Even today, it is forbidden to belong to this society or even display the insignia in Germany.

Victor Schauberger

The information channelled by the Vril society eventually culminated in the construction of the 'Vril Machine'. This was saucer shaped and in addition was allegedly an inter-dimensional time machine, the first piloted flight was reportedly in 1934 and at this point things become confused. One school of thought holds that the information gained from this supposed machine was used in conjunction with the crashed UFO that was discovered in the Black Forest and the resulting data combined with the channelled information from the Vril society, which, in turn, coalesced into the 'Haunebu project'. One aircraft historian, Henry Stevens, claims that the 'Haunebu 1', one of the first attempts at creating one of these remarkable craft, was airborne in 1939 just before the outbreak of the Second World War.

There were many anomalous sighting toward the end of the Second World War including the so-called 'Foo Fighters'. These were luminescent globes of light that accompanied various aircraft in the skies above Germany and no one to this day has any real idea regarding what they were. Some say they were a natural phenomenon of some kind analogous to St Elmo's Fire, but in many cases they seemed to display signs of intelligent control. There were also strange aircraft like the 'Fuerball' and the 'Kugelblitz', which were also credited with flight.

In addition to tales of the fabled Haunebu 1 there were apparently other prototype 'disc craft' around as well, including the designs of talented engineers like Rudolph Schriever, Otto Habermohl and Walter Meithe. The available information suggests that although unconventional in appearance, they were powered by jet engines of various kinds, a bit like the much later US Air Force financed, but Canadian built and ultimately unsuccessful 'Avrocar' which was another disc craft project that almost literally did not get off the ground. In an alternate version of this story, the iconic inventor and scientist Victor Schauberger (1885-1958), also allegedly a Vril Society member, created a number of flying discs between 1938 and 1945. He worked at Mauthausen concentration camp using a mixture of suitably qualified prisoners and German scientists. In a letter allegedly written by Schauberger he gives further information: *"The 'Flying Saucer' was flight tested on the 19th of February 1945 near Prague and attained a height of 15.000 metres in 3 minutes and a horizontal speed of 2,200km/ph. It was constructed according to a Mod 11 design built at Mauthausen concentration camp in collaboration with the first class engineers and stress-analysts assigned to me. It was only after the end of the war that I came to hear through one of the workers under my direction, a Czech, that further intensive development was underway. From what I understand, the machine was destroyed on the direct orders of General Keitel. That's the last I heard of it'.*

Following the end of the war, Schauberger and his son (both speedily removed under Project Paperclip) lived in the USA, where he reportedly worked on an unspecified top secret UFO project in Texas for the US government. It is interesting to note that in some variations on the UFO saga the pilots of these machines are reportedly blond, Aryan types who speak German. The so-called Venusian Saucers, which feature in some abduction accounts, are oddly similar in appearance to original German saucer designs. Considering the influence of Schauberger it is worth a brief digression to examine his work. Even today, his theories still inhabit the areas of 'borderland science'. In this case his researches seem to have involved hitherto unexplored aspects of vortex technology and unusual properties inherent in water.

One of his early designs, and the one that probably interested the Nazis, was a flying device called the 'Climator'. The Climator was eventually refined into the 'Repulsin', which was a circular machine and in many ways was similar to the appearance of the traditional so-called 'Scoutship' vehicles popularised by the notorious supposed 'contactee', the late George Adamski. In this case the power unit was allegedly quite different, because Adamski claimed that the vehicles he encountered (and supposedly travelled in) used some kind of exotic antigravity propulsion system. Schauberger's machines do not appear to have used any form of 'anti-gravitational' device, instead, his technology although still unique was more conventional, relying instead on the diamagnetic properties inherent in rapidly spinning vortices, something that may have resonance with the strange properties claimed for torsion fields and we will look at torsion fields and what they are claimed to do in slightly more detail shortly. The method by which lift was generated in Schauberger's machines used the concept of a turbine spinning and compressing air then expelling it at an extremely high velocity. All of Schauberger's work is allegedly based on entirely natural principles observed by him in everyday life; particularly relating to how water behaves when subjected to a spinning action.

He noticed that water in nature as it flowed in streams, gradually built up spinning vortices that in terms of the energy produced was out of proportion to the external forces that produced the initial vortex. In operation, Schauberger's machine drew air in from the top and expelled it via a unique and complex system of fine vanes to produce a lifting force. The force generated was once again out of all proportion to its input. In essence it is this same system that powers conventional hovercraft and supplies the vectored thrust for certain classes of aircraft; the difference in performance is in the design of the vortex. It is in often claimed, and with good reason, that conventional mainstream science flatly refuses to either recognise or incorporate most fields of borderland physics into its research.

As far as one can see this appears to be due to simple fact that conventional science does not like to have its tidy theories upturned by concepts that it refuses to accept for no better reason that it does not (or will not) understand them. Currently, in some groups Schauberger has achieved an almost mystical, cult-like status similar to that of Nikola Tesla and Guglielmo Marconi. Unfortunately, with the latter two this status derives from contemporary speculation about what they did (or more to the point did not) actually discover.

Make no mistake about it, although responsible for much ground breaking and innovative research, these men, especially Tesla, have had claims and assertions made about their work that is based entirely on sheer speculation mixed with assumption and not a little wishful thinking. Although they were well ahead of their game and tapped into hitherto undiscovered concepts in physics and technology, unless one subscribes to a narrow view encompassing mostly unproven theories, the almost godlike status to which they have been elevated is mostly undeserved.

Die Glocke (The Bell)

Since we have now probed some truly remarkable applications of technology, we should be able now to contemplate at least some of the possibilities and functions attributed to the already mentioned and mysterious 'Die Glocke'. The Bell had originally been located in Berlin and then at the Polish city of Wroclaw, but as the war became increasingly fraught for the Nazi's it was moved again. What is known about this device is sketchy, but the various theories about what it was (and particularly what it supposedly did) appear to be based on a form of technology called 'torsion fields' and the effects they can apparently produce. It is this extremely exotic branch of physics that appears to explain how the aforementioned Victor Schauberger's 'vortex machines' function.We must never forget that conventional science will always try to deny and deflect enquiries into areas that those who work in this field, which is absolutely dominated by very fixed traditions and ideas, have decided are either impossible or not worthy of further investigation.

However the existence of spinning torsion fields might explain telekinesis and levitation plus other paranormal phenomena. This theory suggests that torsion fields might be used to somehow produce working perpetual motion machines, stargates and the propulsion systems used by extraterrestrial spacecraft. As already mentioned, all of these theories are rejected out of hand by current mainstream thinking in the west, but, oddly enough, not in Russia, which is where much of the detailed work on this subject originates. Of course it could well be going on in the USA and elsewhere as well, but subjects like this would be hidden away under the auspices of one black project or another, typically something funded by the CIA whose remit and unique financing, as has already been mentioned, goes much further than one might think.

Torsion field theories are sometimes presented as alternatives to the general theory of relativity. Examples of this include 'Einstein-Cartan Theory', which attempts to include the torsion (or spinning) of space-time with the conventional description of gravity. This, in turn, leads to a whole cluster of unique phenomena including the possibility of time travel. The idea of rotation producing bizarre effects may be more widespread than one might think and one the few western proponents of this is the mathematical physicist and cosmologist, Frank Tippler. Tippler claimed that space/time could be modified by creating a cylindrical body of super-dense material and rotating it. This, he says, would cause space (and therefore time) to be pulled along with it. Unfortunately although theoretically feasible, due to the immense size and bulk of the rotating cylinder this would be impractical, *but it would nonetheless work.*

On another level and in another context, perhaps we should consider that Sufis and Dervishes use a rotating, whirling dance to induce trance states and that the fairies of myth and legend also move in a circular motion while dancing. They are usually depicted as rotating while dancing and moving in a circle; is this part of their 'magickal process' which exploits some unrealised natural phenomenon in much the same way that Victor Schauberger saw the immense potential in spinning water? It seems that many phenomena may be linked by very basic bonds, and once understood are there to be exploited. The Nazi scientists seem to have been able to create the same effect using rotation, but much more effectively. From the little that is known about The Bell, (which is not much) it was around 12 ft high and made of 3 inch thick ceramic material and when in use it emitted a blue glow. For reasons of shielding it was located deep underground; its last place of concealment, the Wenceslas Mine, would have been an ideal location.

It was also filled with a highly radioactive, mercury like liquid metal called Xerum 525 and in this substance were two contra-rotating discs (or cylinders), which were spun at speeds up to 50,000 rpm and would have been the source of the torsion fields. The blue glow, which is often mentioned in reports of how the bell functioned, is in itself is not unusual and is part and parcel of what occurred when old fashioned mercury arc rectifiers were in use. There used to be one in a display case at the Imperial Science Museum in London and the visitors could activate it and see the blue light it emitted. Actually these relatively primitive electrical devices are quite spectacular when in use and if seen out of context by someone who did not know what they were, could easily be taken as something very much, 'not of this earth'. I suppose its rather analogous to the kind of machines that hummed, sparked and crackled as the creature was animated in the early Frankenstein films.

The Xerum 525 may or may not be a variant of another highly unusual metal called 'red mercury' (mercury iodide), but once again there is considerable argument about the validity of its very existence. Other components were rare metals such as Thorium and Beryllium in varying amounts, and copious quantities of high voltage electricity were also needed. Other suggestions are that the Xerum 525 was in fact Beryllium and Thorium suspended in a type of liquid called 'heavy paraffin, which is produced from Deuterium and is something on the same lines as 'heavy water'.

The effects of the radiation it produced were lethal and the device could only be run for a few minutes at a time, but did it really generate a sufficiently strong torsion field to perturb space/time. There is certainly some evidence that time slowed down for anything placed in the immediate radiated field, but one must wonder if it was ever sufficiently developed, or made safe enough, to allow a human being (like *SS* general Hans Kammler) to escape retribution? Even if there was a very real risk of permanent damage to anyone using it, perhaps given his choices Kammler had sufficient confidence in it to actually use it, assuming that is what he did.

The Evidence

As regards just how feasible and viable all this is, the existing reports reflect attitudes prevalent at the time, attitudes created by the level of technology and almost art-deco approach to visions of future science. This approach is evident in the Fritz Lang's classic film *'Metropolis'*, where the majority of people are reduced to the level of machines. A virtual underclass of Wellsian 'Morlocks' created to serve a ruling elite. On a practical level there is little actual hard evidence to support these claims. Other than alleged witness testimony and blurred photographs allegedly depicting flight tests of these UFO's, (there are no actual images of The Bell at all) all that can be stated with any degree of confidence is the following.

A) The Thule and Vril societies did exist
B) Extremely influential members of the Nazi high command were members of – and believers in – the esoteric teachings of these societies.
C) Magick and the occult are strange and mutually self-fulfilling beasts. It has often been said that we create our own reality and perhaps a belief in the occult actually allows it to exist.
D) Himmler was noted as a particularly fastidious man who had no stomach for personal contact with the grisly realities of the death and carnage created by his orders and policies. Therefore it is unlikely that he would have personally been present at the ritual torture of human sacrifices and finally,
E) Presumably Schauberger's letter referring to the 'Flying Saucer' aircraft was written after 1947, because the term Flying Saucer was not generally used prior to this. It was not coined until after the famous Kenneth Arnold multiple UFO sighting at Mt. Rainier in Washington State, USA in 1947. Oddly enough, Arnold never actually used the expression 'flying saucer', although he did describe them as, amongst other things, 'oval', 'convex' and looking like a 'pie plate': in fact some contemporary images show them as looking something like a boomerang. The term 'flying saucer' probably originated with some now unknown sub-editor who created the term based on the descriptions used during the interview. We will return to the Mt Rainier sightings shortly.
F) There was a fully functioning German nuclear programme in operation at that time and once we add all these elements together we have the basis of several possible scenarios.

G)   It is known that at least 60 scientists and technicians who were involved with 'The Bell' were summarily executed by the *SS* to keep whatever knowledge they possessed from being appropriated by the Allies.

Lastly, the truly epoch shattering device called 'The Bell': did it exist and if it did was it capable of doing what it is claimed to do? The books that mention it certainly lend a specious credibility to its existence and the effects of the radiation it emitted are well documented. They suggest that items of animal and vegetable matter placed in the vicinity of The Bell rotted away, but with no corresponding smell of decay and human beings who happened to be within the location soon displayed signs of illness. This suggests that there may be another, more prosaic explanation for The Bell and what it did and this relates to the acknowledged Nazi nuclear programme. Rather than some kind of time machine of exotic propulsion unit, The Bell could equally well have been an accelerator or centrifuge of sorts, almost identical to those used in the process of producing fissile for weapons use.

Added to this was the interest the Nazi's had in the heavy water (deuterium oxide) plant at Vermork in Norway, which had been built by the Norwegians in 1934. We should keep in mind that nuclear weapons did not suddenly spring into existence with the bombs dropped on the Japanese cities of Hiroshima and Nagasaki, but there had been ongoing research into such devices for decades prior to this. In fact as early as 1917, Earnest (later Lord) Rutherford is credited with having split the atom and named an atomic particle, the proton, in the process. It was from these beginnings that the nuclear race began. The Nazis were in control of the Vermork facility from 1940 until it was destroyed by Norwegian commandos and local resistance fighters in 1943. Although originally intended to produce hydro-electric power and fertiliser, the Nazis recognised that its output could be put to rather more sinister ends.

The fact is that centrifuges are part and parcel of the process in manufacturing fissile material and the most recent example of this was in Iran where there are literally thousands of these devices in use while that country continues in is pursuit producing nuclear fuel to power its 'peaceful nuclear energy' programme, their usage at plants located at Natanz are a prime example. More worryingly similar research is conducted in North Korea using identical devices, again for ostensibly and equally worrying so-called 'peaceful reasons'. However, contemporary usage aside, these reports are apocryphal and the hard evidence is simply just not there to support them. It may well be a prime example of disinformation spread for any number of reasons and like all good disinformation it will contain a sprinkling of facts.

In many ways it is similar to belief in God or other divinity. If you believe in one there is one, and it's not a point for debate, and anything that happens, good or bad, can be attributed to it thereby empowering it and so it is with the UFO's of the Third Reich. While the Nazi's (along with Allies) did have some bizarre experimental aircraft, (they even had a jet aircraft powered by coal gas), it is unlikely that a device like this ever existed in the manner much hypothesised over, except perhaps as some highly exotic 'special project'.

Hans Kammler

We should now return to the man at the centre of much of what occurred and the operation of this and other highly classified *SS* run projects, *SS* General Hans Kammler; did he use time travel to thwart the attempts of the allies to bring him to trial for his war crimes? The answer is almost certainly not, he probably escaped using one of the established rat-runs already set up by the *SS* and its sympathisers, or if he did not escape he may have been justifiably killed by partisans, or, as already suggested, the Russians.

It has also been suggested that, like many of his former associates, he committed suicide in 1945 by taking cyanide, but in spite of this there persists the feeling that somehow he managed to escape and his identity and location were successfully and permanently expunged from history. There have been no recorded sightings of him in the way that, for example, the notorious Doctor Joseph Mengele, or Hitler's deputy Martin Bormann were supposedly seen in South America from time to time. Likewise, if he had been spirited away to America under the auspices of Project Paperclip, unlike Werner von Braun, Walter Dornberger and other German scientists he did not emerge there either.

There is one final aspect which may be relevant to the matter, can we really be sure that if such momentous and potentially civilisation changing technology did actually exist, that any of the forces arraigned against the Nazis, if they had discovered it would not have at least tried to make it work for their own ends? Or if the device had been destroyed as part of a belated 'scorched earth' policy, then the next best thing would have been to interrogate and suborn the scientists who had constructed it, or at least those not murdered by the *SS*? It is very easy to assume that for purely altruistic and humanitarian reasons they decided not to open such a dangerous Pandora's Box and either destroyed it, or in the manner of the 'warehouse scenario' used in the Indian Jones movies, simply locked it away safe from prying eyes.

The likelihood is that given the way the military thinks, and at that time of total war, such advanced technology and those who created it would have been quickly appropriated by whichever side got there first. The already mentioned Operation Paperclip was such a project where any and all technology military and otherwise was taken by the victors from the east and west for their own use, and the supposed properties of 'The Bell' was something they would have literally killed each other to possess. Given the vast ideological differences between the then allies, The Bell and its supposed properties would have been used to obtain the ultimate victory against which there was no possible defence and conscience, ethics and morality would not have come into it.

In all fairness I have to say that my own interest in the preceding subject matter stemmed partly from the revelations in Nick Cook's remarkable book, 'The Hunt for Zero Point' and also Alan Bakers equally excellent 'The Invisible Eagle'. There are also several first class web sites (see the notes and sources) devoted to the matter, all are well worth examining. However the truth of the matter, like so much else when dealing with this subject, is a matter of opinion and taste, nevertheless, in spite of the guesswork and speculation there is still, at its core, a glimmer of fascination with what may, not may not, have happened and it is this that keeps us returning to it in the hope that, finally, the truth will emerge.

Nazi Technology and the UFO Enigma

We have frequently mentioned Project Paperclip and the large number of German scientists who, along with their research, ended up in the USA. We have also mentioned Kenneth Arnold and what he saw over Mt Rainier, might there be a connection? As we have seen, the aircraft described by Arnold were depicted as (among the 'pie plate' descriptions), looking like a 'boomerang' or a 'scalloped aerofoil' and there is a picture of Arnold standing beside one of these pictures, so presumably this has some credence. If that is the case, then we should consider the possibility that what Kenneth Arnold saw was an early version of an American 'flying wing': could that be feasible?

Among the designs and technical information taken to the USA under the auspices of Paperclip were a large number of projects being designed by the Horten Brothers who had already produced a workable flying wing with the 'Ho 229', which was a jet powered fighter aircraft captured by the Americans and taken back to the USA. Another of their designs, again a flying wing, was the long-range HoVIII, part of the 'Amerika Bomber' project to create an aircraft that could reach and attack America. It is no accident that the subsequent Northrop flying wings (Northrop was chosen because the company already had some experience in flying wing designs) bear considerably more than a passing resemblance to the Horten design.

The Kecksberg Incident and 'The Bell'

Another genuinely perplexing UFO related encounter that carries echoes of what 'Die Glocke' might have been involves the December 1965 encounter with what is claimed to have been an extraterrestrial spacecraft. This incident was witnessed by several people and members of the local volunteer fire department report that they saw an object the shape of an acorn and about the size of VW Beetle. This would more or less describe the appearance of the The Bell, or something very like it. The outcome was that the state police roped off the area in preparation for the US Army to arrive to inspect what had landed. Despite what the fire department saw, after the army did arrive and the area was duly inspected, they reported that, perhaps predictably, 'nothing was found'.

Another witness to the events was John Murphy, the news director of the local radio station. Murphy was on the scene responding to reports from concerned listeners well before the authorities arrived. He conducted several interviews and took pictures of the object and said that although dark he could see it was 'cone like'. The authorities confiscated his reels of film and as it turned out the audio tapes he made relating to a documentary he had made for his radio station, WHJB, about the incident, He was also visited by two men who looked like stereotypical MIB's and warned to forget everything. In 1969, the unfortunate Murphy was killed by an unidentified vehicle in a hit-and-run accident while on vacation in California. Those responsible for his death remain undetected.

There is also some evidence that what came down, and there is no doubt that 'something' did in fact land, was debris from a crashed Soviet satellite, a Kosmos 96, which had an acorn-like shape. It also reputedly had strange lettering around its outer edge; this was noted by the few people who actually saw it. This claim of having 'strange lettering' around its rim is also attributed to 'The Bell', (as it happens it is also an assertion made for some fragments of debris found at the Roswell crash site).

As one might expect the entire incident became embroiled in claim and counter claim with neither side able to produce convincing evidence regarding the origins or nature of what came down in the woods near Kecksberg, this is still the case five decades later. Was it a spacecraft, was it a Russian satellite, although officially there is no evidence to say that anything man-made entered the atmosphere that day, or might it have been an example of 'Bell' technology being tried? No one knows and it is likely that no one ever will, but as ever with each passing year the legend becomes ever more firmly entrenched in the folklore of Ufology and its occult crossovers. From here it is an easy journey to the very outer edge of what the Nazis might have been doing.

From the Sublime to the Ridiculous…or is it?

If the endless possibilities of the time travel hypothesis which has been associated with The Bell were found to be viable, there is one final aspect of this matter that may be worth exploring. It is a contention that seems to dovetail with the nature of subject and that is the possible existence of a little known and probably fictitious organisation known as the 'Karotechia Group'. A word of warning here, because although this sub-group may never actually have existed in the real world, as we have seen and given the known appetite of senior Nazis (Heinrich Himmler in particular) for the occult and magick it cannot be entirely ruled out. Why, because in parallel with the long running UFO mythos, as we have seen the truth is frequently concealed by a cloak of half truths, misinformation, evasions, denials and downright lies. It is a still ongoing process successfully used for decades by the US (and other) intelligence services to conceal various military and other 'black projects' that may never even come to fruition. For that reason I have included some information about what is known about the Karotechia Group in this chapter.

To be absolutely clear about this, it is entirely possible that this Karotechia Group is purely the creation of the agile intellects that construct the incredibly detailed backgrounds to the sprawling series of war games of various genres that abound on the Internet. In that respect it resembles the notorious and fictitious grimoire, 'The Necronomicon'. This tome was originally created in the mind of the American fantasy (although what he wrote was arguably Science Fiction) author H.P Lovecraft, but which attracted an immense following based on the cosmology he created with his books dealing with creatures emanating from alternate realities in the spaces between the stars.

So much so that it was actually brought into being by several writers (the British author Colin Wilson was one and someone known only by the name, 'Simon', was another and there are a few more) and became a reality simply because it *needed* and *deserved* to be real and made manifest. In fact it should be emphasised that an entire strain of magick developed around it and currently there are several groups dotted around the world devoted to so-called 'Lovecraftian magick', which is based on ancient Sumerian rituals designed to invoke demons. In other words, perhaps if the lure is strong enough these concepts have a habit of becoming real…and if so the Karotechia would be no exception.

According to the story, the Karotechia Group was an offshoot of the *'Ahnenerbe*, which was indisputably real and became incorporated into the *SS* in 1940. The Ahnenerbe was regarded by Himmler as a racial purity and occult research unit within the German military machine and tasked with seeking out the supposed noble and god-like origins of the German people. It existed at the boundaries of what is possible and perhaps even desirable and Hans Kammler, as would befit his inclinations, was supposedly involved. In fact all of the Ahnenerbe staff were members of the *SS,* some of high rank, even if only holding honorary status. In spite of the official 'pooh-poohing' by many authorities, like it or not, many very senior Nazi's *did* have a mystical bent (especially those at the very top) and magick was seen as only another tool that could be used in their battle for supremacy.

The name, 'Karotechia', originated from another secretive organisation called 'Sonderkommando-H'. This small subsection was reputedly designated to collect information from libraries in Austria and Germany concerning the various savage inquisitions orchestrated by the Catholic Church during the Dark and Middle Ages and collate them into a catalogue named 'The Hexenkartothek', (from Hexen, the German word for witch), which eventually contained many thousands of cards containing the names of those implicated in the various European witch trials.

The information gathered by this organisation was originally intended to act as propaganda to justify a crackdown by the *SS* on the Catholic Church; as it later turned out Heinrich Himmler also had special and personal interest in these activities, because he was convinced that an ancient German religion had been subverted because of the prolonged and negative effects of the various inquisitions. Typically of such rarefied groups before and since, and there are plenty of precedents, the *SS* men who gathered this information started calling themselves the 'Kartothekia', and as a bonus the original information they retrieved turned out to be rather more than what they had been seeking. Instead of just names, dates, places, perceived heresies and crimes against the Church, much of what they unearthed described the actual rituals, ceremonies and often Gnostic and alchemical practises used by those accused of witchcraft and heresy.

It is here that events start to take a much more worrying turn because apparently this group went on to actually re-enact and conduct some of these rites and rituals on their own account and began to award themselves the ranks of sorcerer and warlock. The legends associated with the group claim that one of their number, a Haupstscharfurher Dieter Scheel, led a team to successfully resurrect a 17th century magician Jurgen Tess. Following on from this Sonderkommando-H was replaced by the 'Kartothekia', which was now allegedly instrumental in placing their newly found occult talents in the service of the Reich. Again there is much confusion and speculation about what (if anything) really occurred here, simply because the subject has been repeatedly mauled by those who have no desire to see any interest reignited. One can hardly blame them, but as a result of their efforts the entire subject has become conflated into a heaving mass of conjecture also perhaps, just perhaps, some truth.

Although what we know of this 'Kartothekia Group' may be nothing more than a highly plausible work of fiction, there is something else to be considered here and yet another reason why one cannot simply dismiss these stories entirely. The former chief Vatican exorcist, Fr Gabriel Amorth SJ, has stated repeatedly that he considered all of the senior Nazis, especially Adolph Hitler, to be actively and permanently possessed by demonic entities. Fr. Amorth also made the same claim in relation to the psychotic tyranny of Joseph Stalin and given the horrific pogroms orchestrated by these men and their lieutenants who is to say he is wrong? This does of course introduce other, perhaps unwelcome, aspects to what may or may not have occurred, not least the nature of evil and its opposite, good.

Is evil a purely transient electrochemical process created in the human brain, is it something generated by an inhuman, unearthly agency, or is it something that resides latent and hidden in the human psyche, only awaiting the correct set of circumstances before it is set free to wreak its baleful and malign influences on the rest of humanity? If that is the case then is the concept of 'good' an automatic reaction to this and released as an attempt to restore some kind of gnostic or karmic balance? Perhaps we shall never know, but people like Fr. Amorth and his associates see it as caused by, what are to them at least, very real entities that exist quite separately from humanity, but can, in the right circumstances, actively possess certain people…or groups of people.

There is even some suggestion that Pope Pius XII attempted a remote exorcism on Adolph Hitler, although the veracity of this claim cannot be checked. Fortunately, since the universe seems to run on the Gnostic principles of balance, evil is counterbalanced and neutralised by the forces dedicated to positivity and 'good'. In this context both of these words, good and evil, serve as analogues for very real forces and impulses and while what causes them is open to interpretation, the fact remains that they both exist and function whether only as mere concepts or as only too real energies in their own right and that is irrespective of where or how they originate.

This tends to introduce yet another dimension to the mix; the mention of 'psychotic tyranny' employed by both Hitler and Stalin and many other dictators both before and after, the ongoing situation in North Korea is a case in point. Is psychosis a sign of demonic possession or a medical condition that can perhaps be helped by suitable medication? The answer is that it is possible to control the condition, but a psychopathic personality is likely to remain that way, totally devoid of empathy, unemotional, callous, utterly self-centered, but with an incredible capacity to charm and flatter in order to get other people to see things their way. It is possible that many highly successful businesses owe their success to those at the top who display many of the classic signs associated with a psychopathic personality.

Chapter Two:
Truth, Lies and Ufology

Disinformation and Paul Bennewitz

As far as Ufology goes I am regarded as something of a heretic and make no apology for it, this is not because I deny that we are visited by non-human, non-terrestrial entities, but because I don't accept the validity of their point of origin. I also believe that many of the classic sightings of, and encounters with, UFO's and their occupants were either faked in one way or another or were misidentified or did not occur in the manner described (if indeed at all) and I cite the claims made by George Adamski and others of his notorious ilk as a case in point. One of the major problems is that the subject involves a whole slew of interrelated subjects, it is impossible not to. These encompass a combination of the paranormal, conspiracy theory, secret underground bases, the presence of extraterrestrials living here on earth, UFOs, shadowy government agencies, the New World Order, you name it; this is the stuff from which many still extant hard core legends were made.

It is also fair to comment that many of the serious books written about the subject rely entirely on evidence of a highly dubious and speculative nature that has, through time, become accepted as incontrovertible fact. Modern researchers who use the earlier (albeit probably well intentioned) books as a source of reference are quoting evidence that is tainted at best and utterly bogus at worst. When this happens the myth is further reinforced, but no amount of sincerity or force of belief on the part of the proponent will make it true.

In short, I do not accept the reality or viability of the extraterrestrial hypotheses (ETH) for several good reasons. One of these is based (quite apart from why any other race would want to come here) on the sheer distances involved and the length of time required to travel to this planet from whatever location these 'visitors' call home. Unless they have solved many currently insurmountable issues surrounding superluminal travel, then by our understanding of physics they cannot come from nearby star systems, if indeed they originate in this universe at all.

However, it has to be said that the subject matter of this chapter, Paul Bennewitz and how he was cruelly and cynically treated by various U.S. intelligence agencies, has created one of the most enduring and fascinating myths in the entire panoply of Ufology. It is a subject that became so deeply embedded in UFO lore that even today it is still believed that what Bennewitz reported was a factual account of events that actually occurred as he described them. All of this despite admissions of culpability from those who helped spread the rumours and lies upon which Bennewitz constructed his near-apocalyptic views.

This is absolutely symptomatic of a subject entirely mired in paranoia, disinformation, evasions and the machinations of various security services coupled to a desperate need to believe that is greater than the abundant evidence to the contrary. It has been persuasively argued that Ufology is like a form of religion and indeed a few have been founded on some of the precepts, but if it is then the skilfully engineered downfall of Paul Bennewitz shows its darker side. Before actually getting around to looking at the details of the mythology Bennewitz was encouraged to create, it is vital to look at how the world looked then both politically and culturally and it was a very different place to the one we know now.

Opening Shots

There are two early contenders in the modern canon of Ufological belief, one occurred in 1948 when Capt Thomas Mantel crashed his P51 fighter after chasing a supposed UFO above Godman Army Airfield in Kentucky. Later investigations revealed that the UFO was more likely to have been a Skyhook balloon, something still disputed by the 'true believers'. Another was the notorious 'UFO's over Washington' flap, which was not a result of radar returns generated by temperature inversions as was suggested, but a prime example of a clandestine and extremely clever operation instigated by the US Intelligence services called 'Project Palladium'.

Project Palladium was an early manifestation of ECM's (electronic counter measures) designed to create false images on radar screens; images that would zip around those screens in various numbers at various heights and at various speeds. The project was originally designed to train radar operators, but the powers that be quickly realised that it could be better used by the U.S. intelligence services. One idea that developed from this was designed to measure how Russia, or any other perceived foe, (Cuba for example), would deal with incoming hostile aircraft. Experiments using this then cutting edge technology were intended to measure response times taken for fighter squadrons to react or missile batteries to come on line, or the general efficiency of the opposing radar systems could be calculated.

This last measurement was especially revealing, because it also inferred a great deal about the level and development of existing Soviet electronic technology, which the West, rightly or wrongly, assumed to be inferior to its own. In other words this is about madness, paranoia, lies, deception, misinformation, disinformation with perhaps just a grain of truth, all examples of the classic smoke and mirrors methodology surrounding the UFO phenomenon, or at least the ETH version of it. In the midst of this there are of course genuine 'unknowns' in the equation as well, but that is exactly what they are, 'unknown', they are not necessarily non-terrestrial spacecraft and could equally well be electromagnetic anomalies or the result of some still unsuspected 'black' project and there are still plenty of those.

The Secret Underground Bases

Another component in the hard core of Ufology is the belief in the existence of a network of clandestine facilities buried deep underground. One the main contenders in this scenario is Dulce Base and with it the alleged Dulce War, which was supposedly a stand off between ET's and members of an elite US military unit (Delta Force). I will not go into the minutia of this case, because the reader will probably know at least some details about the supposed colonies of ET's hidden there with full knowledge and acquiescence of the US (and other) Government agencies. The ET's were allowed to stay there and conduct alleged genetic experiments in return for allowing the US government access to their supposedly advanced technology, or at least so went the hypothesis.

Remember this is not about the validity or otherwise of UFO's or bases or any of the rest of the subculture and industry that has steadily evolved around Ufology, especially in America. In this case it is about the cynical, calculated destruction and discrediting of one man by the US Government under the aegis of Air Force Office of Special Investigations (AFOSI) simply because his obsession UFOs was seen as a risk (real or perceived) to US security. Maybe this was the beginning of how the US intelligence services started using Ufology and its mythology entirely for its own ends and Bennewitz was their first test subject…their unfortunate guinea pig.

AFOSI

The main instigator of the plan, AFOSI, (sometimes called just OSI), was founded along with much else in 1947 (quite a year that) and was first located at Bolling AFB in Washington State. Its stated aims are to:

1)   Develop and retain a force capable of meeting Air Force needs.
2)   Detect and provide early warning of worldwide threats to the Air Force.
3)   Identify and resolve crime impacting Air Force readiness, or good order and discipline.
4)   Combat threats to Air Force information systems and technologies.
5)   Defeat and deter fraud in the acquisition of Air Force prioritized weapons systems.

Given the stakes that were being played for these aims are entirely reasonable and under this range of responsibilities it became clear that some individuals who had more that a passing interest in UFOs might damage the elaborate cover surrounding many secret projects and were therefore seen as a potential threat to the Air Force and therefore USA.

Since we mentioned that 1947 was quite eventful it might be useful to look at this year in slightly more detail. It was an interesting year that all sorts of reasons and not just for what supposedly happened at Roswell either; although perhaps this coloured much of what subsequently developed. Many key events happed that year, among them:

• The Kenneth Arnold and Mt Rainier sightings.
• Chuck Yeager broke the sound barrier.
• The world's first digital computer, ENIAC, was switched on.

- The transistor and microwave oven appeared.
- The AK47 was introduced.
- The OSS became the CIA (more of that later).

The US Air Force also came into existence; (it was formerly the Army Air Force) and of course no mention of 1947 would be complete without including Roswell.

Finally, it was the year in which Scientology founder Ron Hubbard and the ritual magician and rocket scientist Jack Parsons (with the disapproval of the notorious mage Aleister Crowley) attempted a ritual called the Babylon Working in an effort to open a portal allowing an entity access to our version of reality.

Curiously enough, Hubbard was supposedly involved with naval intelligence at the time, which is another link between the intelligence services and possible risks to security and/or unusual applications of technology; if magick can be classified as technology. All as this should be viewed in the context of the possibility that total war with the USSR and complete nuclear annihilation was still a very real threat, because remember that context is everything here. A very, very risky time indeed, the Cold War still raged, the arms race was rampant, the Soviet Union and the USA were subsuming anything, no matter how unlikely, in an attempt to gain ascendancy over one another. This continued well into the 1980's and includes such remarkable enterprises as the Stargate Project with its teams of remote viewers, the so-called 'PSI spies'. In fact nothing however unlikely was ruled out if any perceived military, propaganda or political advantage could be attained.

Viewed in that context we should understand that yes, the US government has indeed lied consistently about UFO's and what they are, but perhaps not for the reasons you might think. This was not about concealing some dire alien threat because the public would panic and riot; this was about establishing and maintaining the USA as the predominant power in the world. One of the main tools used in this quest was the newly created CIA, which was, as noted, formed in 1947 under the administration of President Harry Truman. This came about when the Office of Strategic Services (OSS) morphed into the CIA under its first director Admiral Sidney William Souers and a whole new era dawned. It is fair to say that in these first years there was little hint of just what a Frankenstein's monster had been awakened

For next three decades this organisation tried to dominate the world. Its budget was virtually unlimited and for long period of time some analysts say it was out of, and possibly beyond, control. Perhaps the organisation considered that it was at the forefront of protecting America and with it the entire West from the perceived predations of communism and like the computer, HAL, in the groundbreaking film '2001 A Space Odyssey' the responsibility made it unstable. Again to use the HAL analogy, because of the general insecurity in the world the director of CIA became accountable only to himself and his mission.

In this era of coercion, assassination and attempts to control how the rest of the world thought, sometimes literally through attempts at thought control, the CIA and their Russian counterparts the KGB did everything in their power to win the proverbial hearts and minds in every country they thought might serve their respective agendas. If ever there was a secret, i.e. a covert government within a government pulling the strings it was this. The era also saw the CIA's involvement and active participation in the birth of the concept of psychological operations (PSYOPS), and mind control experiments like the horrendous and destructive MK ULTRA At one time due to rigid compartmentalisation, there were so many CIA authorised projects ongoing that almost no one knew what the CIA was doing, not even the US president and perhaps not even the director himself.

While all this was proceeding apace, yet another government body was created under the Truman presidency. In 1951 the Psychological Strategy Board (PSB) sprang into being with the aim of projecting and presenting the American way of life as a universal standard and a kind of idealised Heaven on earth. The PSB worked hand in glove with CIA in promoting the USA and its interests worldwide and they complimented each other. They adopted the policy that the United States of America and individual Americans should conform to specific standards in how they behaved, acted and thought; this was, perversely, something that might have come right out of Orwell's nightmare vision of the future laid out in his book, the strangely, perhaps frighteningly, prophetic and dystopian, '1984'.

In fact Orwell's created a language called 'Newspeak' which included such terms as 'unperson' and 'crimethink' and was used by the regime that ruled in his novel to help stifle individuality and freedom of thought. This has perhaps already come to pass in terms of the strangulation of free speech that has already occurred under the umbrella of knee jerk political correctness. When one adds the fact that there are already groups in place that seem determined to invent new categories of 'thought crime' ('Thoughtpol' was another of Orwell's Newspeak definitions and refers to the 'thought police') and the number of intrusive CCTV cameras that monitor almost all of our actions then it seems that in some ways Orwell was much too close for comfort. This is where we should be extremely circumspect about what we regard as a democracy. The west is supposedly a democracy, but if you look closely it is not. Here in the UK we live in a parliamentary democracy, which is not the same thing. In fact a true democracy, like true communism, is much too unwieldy and unworkable. Winston Churchill once said that *'Democracy is the worst form of government except for all the other forms that have been tried from time to time.* A concept that was and indeed still is absolutely correct in the supposedly 'free' west.

As its influence grew, in 1952 the PSB took over the CIA's own psychological operations programme and in 1953 changed its name to the more anodyne 'Operations Coordinating Board'. From then until the 1970's the CIA went on its way unhindered by any concept of ethics; however there was one set of rules it had no choice other than to follow. Under the National Security Act it could not conduct activities like assassinations etc, within the continental United States. Bearing in mind what has already been implied about skulduggery and conspiracy theory: in 1962, after the disastrous Bay of Pigs fiasco, another operation was planned by the CIA when they instigated Operation Northwood, which was a classic false flag operation whereby mainland USA would be bombed and the blame put on Cuba.

As far as UFO phenomenon was concerned, in 1953 the CIA formed the Robertson Panel whose brief was to monitor and infiltrate various UFO groups, the now defunct Aerial Phenomena Research Organization (APRO) founded in 1952 by Jim and Coral Lorenzen was one such, with a view to either help spread disinformation or see just what these groups were monitoring regarding classified weapons and technologies. It also continued to conduct a range of destabilising operations until, in 1973, in face of fierce resistance, Senator Frank Church set up a committee to investigate the organisation. This resulted in the CIA admitting to a much wider range of manipulation that at first thought, not only abroad but particularly in the US media at all levels.

Paul Bennewitz and His Role

This kind of activity is one thing, but what has this to do with UFOs and Paul Bennewitz? The answer is pretty much everything, because it shows how these agencies work, especially when they finally turned their attention to UFO's and how this could be exploited to the USA's military advantage. They did this in the full knowledge that it could be done in various ways; they could set out false trails about the sophistication of American technology and hide what they were doing by deliberately feeding false information to those who took the subject of UFOs seriously.

I'm old enough to remember when it was common for the speakers at UFO conferences to welcome the audience and add a special welcome for anyone from the intelligence community who might also be there, because in most cases they were…and perhaps still are. Why? To both see just how well their disinformation was doing and also see if anyone had perhaps sighted something in the skies that just might just belong to a foreign power, most likely the USSR as it was at the time…or possibly something home built. So it is obvious that the intelligence community had good reason to feed the UFO faithful with what they wanted to hear and supply any 'evidence' as required to maintain that level of belief.

This evidence normally came in the form of leaked documents and other paperwork relating to sightings and other aspects of the phenomenon and of course the classic MJ12 dossier is a prime example of that. As far as Paul Bennewitz is concerned, there nothing out of ordinary about him, he was an electronics expert with interest in UFO's, or perhaps more than an interest, more of a fixation and it was his ultimate and tragic undoing. He had created an electronics company called Thunder Scientific, a small defence contractor that made specialist equipment for NASA and US Air Force. The man was highly intelligent, basically decent and possessed of a rare tendency: patriotism.

He lived not far from Kirtland AFB and around 1979 started out checking reports of cattle mutilations and also alien abduction in the area, he interviewed several of the claimants and this was what first created his abiding interest in the subject. Before moving on, the idea of cattle mutilation, or 'mutes', was also supposedly part of the government plan to allow ET's access to tissue samples from cattle etc. People who claim to have seen this occur (it was always at night) frequently claim there were odd lights in the sky accompanied a strange buzzing or humming noise from overhead while this was going on.

It was at around the same time that missile silos in various American states attracted visits from what were supposed to be UFO's in the form of balls of light hovering in the sky above the silos. There were also reports that sometimes the electronics in the missiles malfunctioned. The servicemen charged with guarding these facilities were specifically instructed not to fire on these balls of light or shine lights on them, one must ask why? The answer is because the 'balls of light' were not extraterrestrial, but were extremely specialised but completely terrestrial devices: they were all examples of the Hughes 500P helicopter, sometimes called 'The Quiet One'.

These helicopters had highly specialised main and tail rotors, had silencers fitted to their exhaust and inlet manifolds and had highly efficient sound absorbent cladding on the fuselage. They were also fitted with the first generation of infra-red night vision optical equipment, precursors of the much improved devices now fitted to Apache Longbow attack helicopters and other stealth aircraft. More importantly, they were also deliberately equipped with strange lighting configurations designed to make them appear as glowing balls of light. In their more 'conventional' roles they were used by the CIA for various clandestine duties, but there is no doubt that they (or something very like them) were also used as a means of promoting the UFO myth.

Bennewitz also began making home movies of lights in sky above the nearby Kirtland/ Manzano area. He traced this UFO/ET activity to the vicinity of the Archuletta Mesa on Jicarilla Apache Reservation land near the town of Dulce. He also used his extensive electronic knowledge to construct receivers capable of allowing him to monitor communications at the Manzano mountain range (which is one location of the US govt weapons contactor Sandia Labs). At the time Sandia, part of Lockheed-Martin, was overseen by the US Dept of Defence which gives an indication of its key position within the intelligence community.

The Manzano range also concealed one of the largest depositories of nuclear weapons in the USA if not the world. Bennewitz investigated further and became convinced of the existence of underground bases where ET designated experiments were conducted. Especially the subterranean base supposedly concealed deep under Dulce; in fact almost the entire Dulce Base legend stems from the speculations of Paul Bennewitz. Let me explain that I have no issue with underground bases, of course there are hidden research and command facilities locate all over the world, I would be surprised if there were not and I have visited one currently open to the public near St Andrews in Scotland. They were required for national security and have nothing to do with ET and I doubt if they ever have; although they would admittedly have made ideal hiding places.

In 1980, after carefully collating what he had gathered, Bennewitz submitted his evidence to the authorities at Kirtland Air Force case, following which he was formally invited to the facility to address senior staff. As far as he was concerned it was his duty to alert officials running the various departments to the possibility that ET's were monitoring and recording the activities both there and the surrounding area. From the perspective of Bennewitz these signals represented were a real threat to the nearby Manzano Nuclear Weapons Storage Area and by implication the security of the entire USA.

The meeting duly took place but unfortunately most of those present found that Bennewitz's evidence, although highly detailed was unlikely and the only organisations who took an interest were AFOSI and the NSA. These two bodies realised that what he thought were ET transmission were in fact their own. Following this meeting AFOSI (and the NSA) realised that they had to find out the extent of Bennewitz's knowledge and became directly involved in investigating the extent of what he knew and with whom he was sharing it. This eventually led to what is now generally acknowledged as a deliberate disinformation campaign to discredit Bennewitz and simultaneously safeguard national security interests.

Dulce Base

Let's pause for a moment to look at Dulce, although it has to be said that most of what is claimed is founded on no more than hypothesis, speculation and assertion created initially by Paul Bennewitz and latterly with the assistance and disinformation put out by the NSA and AFOSI. According to the accepted UFO/ET based version of events, in 1933 the US government acknowledged the presence of an alien presence on the North American Continent and they entered into an agreement with the aliens to exchange animals and humans for advanced technology. Although Dulce Base was not constructed until 1947 the aliens were allowed undisturbed use of other bases elsewhere in the western United States.

Neither is the choice of these areas accidental, according to Greg Bishop who is another well known American UFO researcher and sometime historian, the ET's deliberately chose the areas due to their unique geological placements. Bishop goes into considerable detail about the methods used to construct Dulce Base and its alleged 'tube tunnel' system, insisting that many of these tunnels were constructed by specially designed machinery that literally melted the rock as it proceeded through allowing the molten rock to harden and vitrify into smooth walls.

I have to express some serious doubts and reservations about this, not about the machine *per se* because tunnelling machines are relatively commonplace, but how this one was claimed to operate. Melting rock that sets as it passes along? Really? The temperatures produced would be incredible and the machine would have to be amazingly robust and extremely well insulated; how would it melt and vitrify the rock then stop it from setting around it? However, this is typical of the assertions and speculation that, over the years, has grown around the Dulce story.

The entire Dulce facility is/was allegedly a Genetics Laboratory linked through a network of vitrified tunnels to the LANL (Los Alamos National Laboratory) by the previously mentioned tube shuttle system. The area surrounding the town and base supposedly has an ongoing extremely high incidence of UFO sightings and according to various reports the location is a nexus of various phenomena both natural and otherwise. The base is supposedly constructed on several levels around a central hub, which is the security section, the deeper you go the stronger the security, there are reportedly (and unsurprisingly) thousands of video cameras situated within the complex covering all high security areas. According to a former (typically unnamed) employee, the deepest sections of the complex connect with natural fissures and caverns. This employee, who had an impressive sounding 'Ultra 7' security clearance, reported that there were more than seven levels incorporating accommodation for both human and ET's. The employee also claims that there is one particular level, the sixth, nicknamed 'Nightmare Hall' and it is there that the genetics labs (and presumably their products) were situated.

Recently the announcement was made that the lengthy and complex Human Genome Mapping Project had been successfully concluded, however, according to reports from Dulce this was achieved here many years ago. This type of information was at the crux of what fascinated Bennewitz and is absolutely typical of the type of enticing information fed to him. The mythology also claims that various means of mind control are in constant use there to keep the population in check. This ties in with known projects involving previously mentioned CIA sponsored mind control experiments like Project Artichoke and ending with the notorious MK-SEARCH and MK-ULTRA. All were funded over a period of almost thirty years and although all these projects were allegedly scrapped in 1973, it is generally accepted that they still continue, although deeply hidden away behind different names and black budgets.

Because of its unique role in the political and security arrangements of the USA, the record of agencies like the CIA is littered with suppressed accounts of secret experiments carried out on the public in, as they saw it, the interests of national security. There is likewise a consensus of opinion that the majority of reports concerning alien abductions and implants are based in clandestine projects orchestrated by various intelligence services of one kind or another. It is as well to point this out because, typically, the 'smoke and mirrors' secrecy employed by the intelligence community is helped considerably by the attitude of the various groups watching them. The CIA and NSA are aware of the rampant paranoia existing within UFO groups, who in turn are aware of similar tendencies in those organisations, it is a truly vicious circle of claims, counter claims, assertions and inevitably yet more disinformation.

Staying with Dulce Base, the aforementioned Greg Bishop reported that there were more than 18,000 non-terrestrials located there and in late 1979 there was a confrontation allegedly involving loaded weapons being carried by both sides inside the base. Although neither the humans nor Ets would permit the other to be armed this eventually ended up in another classic episode in the UFO legend i.e. the Dulce War. It is a part of the equation worth mentioning, because it almost certainly did not occur, or if it did it was a misquoted or misunderstood account of something quite unrelated. As was said at the start, much of the UFO/ET mythos of this era is based on similar tales that had their roots in the ingenious plots and seductive disinformation being peddled by the intelligence agencies.

Another noted known UFO researcher who became involved was William (Bill) Moore who worked in direct collaboration with Doty and others in AFOSI and the NSA. He was knowingly feeding false information and disinformation to the ever eager and gullible Bennewitz. Moore in turn was convinced that for doing this he was being made privy to the real information with privileged access to genuine documentation. Both he and Bennewitz were dupes and completely drawn in by the elaborate deception. Never assume that the intelligence agencies are incompetent, for they are not: Moore and Bennewitz WANTED the truth to be out there and the intelligence agencies ensured that their desires were fulfilled.

Project Aquarius and MJ12 were of course all part of the elaborate (albeit convincing) combined CIA/NSA disinformation campaign.

The saddening thing is that while addressing the 1989 MUFON conference Moore actually publicly admitted his role in the Bennewitz affair and many of the audience were in tears at what they regarded as a shameful example of duplicity. He also suggested that Richard Doty was only a bit player as well, dancing to the tune of others much higher up the chain of command. However many hard core UFO adherents, true to the tenets of their beliefs, refused to accept what he said assuring themselves (and each other) that this was yet another example of the disinformation campaign of concealment at work and a sure sign that 'they' were trying to deflect them from the truth.

One such, Project Aquarius, was the first document that mentions the notorious Majestic/ Majic 12 or MJ 12 committee created from a selection of top level politicians, scientists and personnel from the military to facilitate communication with non-terrestrial races; the proverbial 'first contact' scenario. Aquarius was basically about the protocols to be observed between human and ET's should it ever occur and it has to be said that what it contained was eminently sensible and might serve as a wish list should a real encounter ever occur. It would certainly serve us much better that an all-out armed confrontation that could end in absolute disaster, and not just for the country involved. The document had the effect of increasing the level of Bennewitz's delusion and the outcome was that in 1983 he created Project Beta, his contribution to the already convoluted subject of Ufology.

Richard Doty

What do we know about Richard Doty? He is a genuinely enigmatic character who was deeply involved with the UFO community; ostensibly as an altruist keeping them aware of what was really going on as regards the US government, but in reality he was feeding them well-crafted disinformation hatched by the intelligence services. Doty was involved with AFOSI from late 70's to mid 80's, which was arguably the height of modern UFO mania. As a special agent for AFOSI (which was effectively the USAF version of the FBI) he was stationed at Kirtland AFB hence his involvement with Bennewitz. Doty's actions were eventually exposed and he ended up, still with AFOSI, in West Germany from where he retired from the Air Force and for a time became a New Mexico state trooper. He still regularly appears at UFO conventions in the USA.

Finally, what became of Paul Bennewitz? Well, from the outset this poor man did not enjoy the best mental health and had been treated to the point of hospitalisation for paranoia without any need for UFO input. However the final straw came when he became obsessed with what he thought he was monitoring. The additional pressure heaped on him by Richard Doty and William Moore pushed him right over the edge and he became ever more delusional and paranoid. He claimed that ET's were emerging from the walls of his house during the dark hours and injecting him with unknown chemicals.

He began keeping guns and knives all over his home, until finally in 1988 his health had deteriorated to the point where his business was being run by his sons and he accused his wife of being under the control of ET's. Around this time he decided to sandbag himself into the house, which swiftly led to his hospitalisation suffering from what was euphemistically called "exhaustion". Happily he eventually did recover, but flatly and entirely sensibly broke off all contact with UFO's and Ufology. He died on June 3rd 2003 aged seventy three and over that period in the 1980's had, due to the callous manipulation of the intelligence agencies, almost single handed produced one of the most creative and long lasting episodes in the entire mythology of UFO's. Poor, misused, abused, derided and deluded Paul Bennewitz, RIP.

Chapter Three
Dark Days at Plum Island:
Government Research and Hybrids.

For decades, numerous sightings of strange and anomalous entities have emerged based on whispered reports from secret military installations, or at least restricted areas that are under governmental control. Despite how much security the military employs, every time one of these installations is built and commissioned somehow these sightings still occur, which draws considerable unwanted attention to what actually goes on there. When this happens and curious members of the pubic start taking an interest quite naturally the number of sightings increase, then gradually die away, but crucially never entirely cease.

In common with the extended and extremely successful disinformation campaigns still waged by the various military organisation (and their intelligence community based clones) designed to conceal highly sensitive weapons programmes, some of these sightings are almost certainly the result of already discussed misinformation and disinformation campaigns. As we have seen, these hoaxes are instigated by the authorities to disguise both the nature of the work conducted at these facilities and discredit any reports of sightings of strange or anomalous events; the technique is extremely effective and because of that still ongoing.

Although some of the sightings are likely to be stage managed hoaxes, others may be fleeting glimpses of the end results of ethically flawed and morally dubious experiments conducted there and what is sometimes seen could be very real indeed. This chapter takes a look at a few such areas and while it can offer no definitive answers, it does help to refocus attention on an often neglected backwater of research which is rife with speculation and where the normal, the paranormal (and occasionally, I suspect, the blatantly paranoid) sometimes overlap. I should be very clear that while the information in this chapter mainly applies to the UK and the USA, it can undoubtedly likewise apply to all the major powers, especially Russia and China from where information is much less forthcoming but are equally culpable. Another thing this chapter does is introduce the reader to some worrying trends in social and commercial media, plus some of the darker aspects of the human psyche and what it is capable of, however what it does not knowingly do is judge, only reports on what is already there.

In these relatively sophisticated and supposedly peaceful times, the subject of warfare and the tools used to wage it have become the subject of much discussion; the aim seems to be making it an extremely selective, calculated and almost clinical exercise. In fact the title of an album made by the thrash metal band, 'Cradle of Filth,' ironically entitled, *'Peace Through Superior Firepower'*, or perhaps instead of Superior Firepower that should really be *'fear'*, just about sums up the situation. It precisely mirrors the strange and fraught days of the Cold War and was referred to by the acronym, M.A.D, or 'Mutually Assured Destruction', which, despite all the lamentations and hand wringing, in its own perverse way actually worked. It had to, simply because the alternatives were simply far too apocalyptic and awful to contemplate. However, of all the tools in the demonic arsenal of war, perhaps more terrifying and certainly considerably more insidious than the ravening cataclysm of a nuclear holocaust, are the so called 'bio-weapons', and, as we shall see, the attendant, hidden abominations deliberately produced through both genetic experimentation and accidents.

Bio-weapons and chemical weapons are far from new; they have been around literally for millennia and were employed in various guises. The use of chemical weapons seems to have started with the Spartans somewhere around 420BC with the use of 'arsenic smoke' and some centuries later with the Greeks when they used 'Greek Fire', (strictly speaking a thermal weapon) and a concoction made from raw petroleum, pitch, sulphur and various resins. Other ingenious methods, unlikely though it may seem, involved the use of prostitutes riddled with various sexually transmitted diseases who were paid to fraternise with the enemy and infect them. In slightly more modern times, and with a certain degree of dark humour, these women were metaphorically termed 'fire-ships' after the old naval practise of setting carefully prepared hulks ablaze and sending them directly into closely massed enemy fleets with the intention of setting them on fire too.

A similar method involved using people who were ill from a range of other highly infections diseases once again passing among the enemy and hopefully infecting them with whatever ailment they had, and the more unpleasant the better. During sieges, rather than the lengthy wait for attrition and starvation to take effect, decomposing animal carcasses were hurled over the walls of whatever redoubt was providing safe haven using catapults of one kind or another, i.e. ballistas and trebuchets. Sometimes rotting animals were not used and buckets of raw faeces were hurled instead, but the purpose was always the same, to weaken the opposition by making them ill, or better yet, killing them.

Bio-weapons

However times and technology changed and so did the methods until, especially during the First World War, a first generation of chemical weapons was devised using mustard, chlorine, phosgene and even cyanide gases. However, the use of cyanide was rapidly halted when it proved as dangerous to those using it as the intended victims. In spite of hastily introduced gas masks and other forms of protection, the remaining gases were extremely and frighteningly effective and were employed by all sides.

As is the way while perfecting warfare, continual refinements in the methods to produce these (and other) gases were made, but in spite of this a measure of sanity still prevailed and during the Second World War poison gas was not normally deployed. That said, when any weapon is deemed effective it is never actually put totally beyond use, i.e. it cannot be 'un-invented' so alternatives were developed. This included toxins such as Ricin, botulism, Sarin, several strains derived from fungi (mycotoxins) and of course the better known anthrax was developed too (and sometimes actually used) after finally being weaponised.

Most countries became involved in this research to a greater or lesser degree after WWII, because the use of these agents as weapons was well recognised. It is worth noting that some of these toxins are worryingly – almost frighteningly-easy to make, especially Ricin, which is produced from the humble castor-oil bean. One fairly recent example of the deliberate use of Ricin was when the dissident Bulgarian journalist Georgi Markov was assassinated on a London street. This was achieved by someone using a weapon disguised as an umbrella to inject a pellet of the toxin into his body. It is thought that agents connected to the Bulgarian secret police carried out the assassination.

A more recent variation on this was the murder in 2006 of a former Russian federal security officer Alexander Litvinenko, who was poisoned by causing him to inadvertently consume the radioactive element polonium 210. Litvinenko, who had been granted political asylum in the UK and was apparently working with MI5 and MI6, had visited a sushi bar with two associates including a so-called 'nuclear expert', and had a meal accompanied by a cup of tea: it was the tea that contained the deadly polonium 210, apparently 200 times the median lethal dose.

In fact the unfortunate Litvinenko died three weeks later bedridden in hospital with his organs in total failure due to acute radiation poisoning: he was doomed as soon as the substance entered his system. The physicians who treated Litvinenko said this was the first time of which they were aware that a murder had been committed in such a manner and the incident ushered in a new era of nuclear terrorism. The 'crime' committed by Litvinenko was his outspoken and unremitting criticism of the Russian security services and that they had orchestrated acts of terrorism to bring Vladimir Putin to power. The man accused of the murder, Andrei Lugovoy, is currently in Russia and a member of the Duma (part of the government) where he enjoys immunity from prosecution.

In the 21st century there have been several instances where US politicians have had letters and parcels containing home made Ricin delivered to them. Rather worryingly it is known that terror groups like Al Qaeda have experimented with this toxin simply because the others are much more difficult to manufacture. At the time of writing this book, investigations (and recriminations) were ongoing in Syria regarding the indiscriminate use of nerve agents in that conflict, with both sides blaming one another. The end result was that the USA and Russia entered into an arrangement to remove and destroy any substances found and also the equipment used for making them. Fine as far as it goes, but of course there would be no guarantee that all the stocks etc would be surrendered and breathtakingly hypocritical since the both 'referees' have their own abundant supplies of chemical weapons. As I said earlier it is always tempting for nations to retain effective weapons and strangely enough, for all its relative size, Syria has (or had) the largest stock of chemical weapons in the world, the USA and Russia included!

Porton Down

Active research in the UK began in 1916 at Porton Down, in Wiltshire, England, (yes, it's been there that long) where, as we have seen, a whole range of relatively primitive substances were developed during World War I, but, with the outbreak of World War II, this reached a whole new level of sophistication. To test the efficacy of some of these compounds, initially at least, the Scottish island of Gruinard was selected and one variety of bio-weapon, anthrax in particular, was used. This deadly toxin was introduced here mainly because the tiny offshore island had been uninhabited since 1920 and therefore monitoring the effects was unimpeded by the need to safeguard any human beings. The tests began in 1942 using a particularly aggressive and virulent weaponised strain of anthrax called *'Vollum 14578'*, which was named after the Oxford professor who developed it, a dubious honour indeed. A number of sheep were taken to the island and tethered while small bombs filled with anthrax spores were detonated.

The sheep (between sixty and eighty of them, the accounts vary) in the test groups began to die within a few days. These tests were filmed and the results classified for decades, they were finally declassified 1997. While confinement to the island (approximately a mile offshore) was intended as an effective form of isolation, its effects may also have been seen on the mainland and the deaths of several farm animals suffering from anthrax-like symptoms were recorded. The outbreak was attributed to the carcass of an infected sheep being washed over to the mainland on a high tide. The island remained off limits, again for decades, and after a decontamination process begun in 1988, was only deemed fit for human beings a year later in 1989.

The decontamination process was carried out by a private contactor and involved the removal of tons of topsoil plus the injection of hundreds of gallons of diluted formaldehyde under what remained. However the wartime project raised many serious doubts about the long term hazards associated with anthrax and made its use on Germany (its intended target) problematic, so ultimately it was never used. Nevertheless, the idea of biological warfare still had its attractions using various short-term nerve gasses etc, so Porton Down was renamed with the relatively innocuous and nondescript title of *'Defence Science and Technology Laboratory (Dstl)'*.

Here various extremely exotic and incredibly toxic substances were developed, along with a whole range of countermeasures and antidotes against them. The justification was much the same as the need for nuclear deterrent, viz. that since the enemy had them we needed them too, apparently the idea of M.A.D has deep roots. However, it may be that the research had unintended side effects and involved deliberately mutated biological organisms and the introduction of an extremely secret series of long term 'deep black' experiments designed, in one instance, to produce what could I suppose be called a 'super soldier'. In this respect according to a 2002 report from the Animal Welfare Advisory Committee of the Ministry of

Defence, pigs were used to help develop specialised protective armour to help prevent injury to the human thorax.

This unlikely asset, the much mythologised 'super soldier', was attempted through a mixture of physical and psychological conditioning assisted by various chemicals and specialised weaponry. As always many of these procedures were initially tested on animals, all of which were eventually supposedly destroyed, but it has been noted by several interested parties that the area of Salisbury surrounding Porton Down is also a hot-spot for UFO (and entity) related sightings. There is justifiable speculation that the unspoken products of the research at Porton Down may well be responsible for some, if not all, of the strange sightings in the area. Keep in mind that in this context these sightings only apply to Porton Down, but as we will see can equally be applied to other facilities worldwide engaged in the same dubious activities.

One such report dating from 2008 was the hotly debated Berwyn Mountain UFO sighting, the occupants of the alleged UFO (which is said to have crashed) were supposedly taken to the facility at Porton Down because of its rigid isolation protocols and of course the correspondingly high level of security in place. This all ties in neatly with earlier accounts dating from 1964 concerning another reputed UFO crash, this time close to Penkridge, a town near the notoriously and abundantly haunted Cannock Chase in Staffordshire, England. Again the wreckage plus occupants were spirited off under a cloak of tight security to Porton Down. Appropriately enough Cannock Chase has a long association with the supernatural and generates regular accounts of werewolves, witchcraft and black magick; a British version of Bigfoot has also supposedly been sighted there.

Before considering the implications of the destruction (or otherwise) of test animals and the possibility that the occupants of a crashed UFO were taken there, there are many highly unpleasant details concerning Porton that normally fail to surface. Some revelations about what went on there strongly imply that somewhere in the region of 20,000 British servicemen (and no doubt women to map possible variations in results due to gender) were duped into volunteering for experiments there under the impression that they were taking part in a project to cure the common cold.

While there may well have been a token number of legitimate experiments to justify this cover story, in fact the majority of those who passed through were exposed to many noxious substances, including nerve gasses and incapacitating agents like CS gas and its many unpleasant derivatives. None of this was, or still is, admitted by the UK armed forces or government, one only has to consider the cover-ups that ensued over 'Gulf War Syndrome' that seems to have been the result of injections using compounds designed to protect servicemen and women serving in that conflict. Exactly what they were being protected against is still far from clear, but almost certainly was a precaution against the use of possible chemical weapons and other nerve agents thought to have been deployed by Saddam Hussein.

One of the more exotic toxic agents tested at Porton Down was *Kyasanur Forest Monkey Disease*, and in 1968 forty individuals were injected with a strain of this disease, the ploy here was that it might have had some therapeutic value in the treatment of leukaemia. Well maybe, e.g. the legitimate medical use of poisonous, natural substances like curare was the result of similar tests, but this disease also has a fatality rate of around twenty eight percent and only eight years later the self same agent became a recognised bio-weapon. Was this only a coincidence, or was there a much more sinister agenda afoot? As far as the reports of any ET's from a downed spaceship being taken there, that is anyone's guess, but given the convoluted reports of what occurred to the occupants of the craft that allegedly crashed at Roswell (yet another tangled, multi-layered and probably insoluble enigma) it cannot be ruled out.

The International Space Station (ISS)

Might these programmes also involve the ISS? This is not all that far fetched and gains some relevance and credibility when one factors in reports that, resonating nicely with the vaguely 'X' Files type claims that the debris from crashed extraterrestrial spacecraft have been taken there, reputedly 'alien' viruses have also reputedly been evaluated. Actually, when one thinks about it that possibility opens up a whole can of worms about manufacturing the ultimate bio-weapon. Small wonder that almost forensic care is taken when manufacturing spacecraft here on earth so that contamination is kept to an absolute minimum. But what if it is not, what if there is a covert plan to send live experimental viruses on space missions to see if they spontaneously mutate once they are off Earth? Again this has basis in fact, where numerous experiments on the ISS have been conducted already and various experiments were conducted off-earth in zero gravity conditions just to see what would happen.

This occurs on a regular (i.e. daily) basis on the International Space Station, where experiments in physics, biology, human biology and also, crucially, on viruses are carried out. In most cases the results of these experiments, which are conducted on behalf of various agencies in the public and private sectors, are no doubt legitimate, but these are the ones that are admitted to. Besides, it is highly likely that the ISS personnel conducting these experiments have no real idea of the purposes to which the end results will be put; it's all about their 'need to know'. It is often suggested that the ethical values of the scientists involved in manning the ISS would inhibit them from participating in anything they regarded as morally repugnant. That being the case it is in the interests of whoever organises (or pays for) the experiments to conceal their real purpose, or indeed hide any suspect elements among the legitimate and beneficial.

In fact, as far as the ultimate isolation technique goes, a module orbiting the earth is about as good as it gets and if something does go badly amiss, then, should the space station experience a catastrophic 'accident' and enter the earths atmosphere everything would (or should) be incinerated. Whether or not this would apply to a mutated virus is a moot point though, since they are notoriously difficult to destroy. Prospects such as that are extremely worrying and absolutely not beyond the efforts of any country with the will and determination to gain ascendancy over its neighbours, but would any country actually do this, i.e. deliberately cause the ISS to crash? Given that the early days of space exploration in the USSR were shrouded in mystery with reports that many of the early Cosmonauts simply 'vanished', such a possibility cannot be ruled out. The remains of one of these unfortunate men reputedly left the solar system some years ago in a capsule that went off course.

As far as UFO sightings at secret installations are concerned, in a parallel with what has been seen (and photographed etc) by astronauts and cosmonauts since the beginning of manned space flight, dozens of UFO sightings have been made by those who crew the ISS. There was quite a flurry of these at the beginning of 2013 and they are readily available on the 'net. In most instances they are images of objects zipping through the upper atmosphere at extremely high speed. There are also images of other objects apparently leaving the atmosphere, again at very high speed; however, the most interesting are those of glowing objects moving against the inky blackness of space. Yes, they are UFOs in the literal sense, but are they extraterrestrial spacecraft? That is an entirely different question, but one that also holds true of UFO sightings in general, including those witnessed at ground based facilities.

The reports of deformed creatures, however, are an entirely different matter altogether and there have been repeated reports of strange creature sighted in the area surrounding Porton Down, especially on the expansive military training areas located on Salisbury Plain. Of the anomalous reports that have emerged from this area many have centred on Warminster, the iconic, almost legendary Wiltshire town that has, over the years, played host to a series of remarkable sightings of both UFOs and bizarre creatures. There is of course the perfectly reasonable argument that the sightings stem from the various, secret military exercises on the nearby Plain, but nonetheless they have been persistent and the possibility that Porton Down has played its part cannot be dismissed. Perhaps something as basic as the simple fact that the scientists, the military and of course the government mandarins and paymasters, will want to play with their new toys. Would they risk the safety of both servicemen and the public to do this? The answer is yes, they would, because it's the only effective way they can evaluate just what their 'toys' will do in a real life situation.

Plum Island

While all this relates to the UK and what occurs in installations sited there, there were (and still are) other instances where tests have been carried out at British controlled installations elsewhere in the world, but as one might imagine in terms of sheer scale the USA, as in most areas is much, much bigger, although not necessarily any better. There are several installations devoted to the development of bio-weapons technology, but none more so than the innocuously named 'Plum Island'. The island, which is located a couple of miles from Long Island and six miles from the Connecticut coastline, was named appropriately enough for its numerous groves of plum trees, but it is for its rather more sinister associations that it became truly notorious.

This eight hundred and forty acre island, which is ostensibly owned by the US Department of Agriculture, played host to another euphemistically titled establishment; *'The Plum Island Animal Disease Research Centre'*. The reason this location was chosen was for the technically correct reason that infectious diseases could be examined without actually being on the US mainland. This seems to be a similar justification to that used for Gruinard Island, but as always the risk, albeit small, for contamination still exists and may take the form of infected soil from the island being washed out to sea and being deposited on an adjacent mainland beach.

On Plum Island so-called 'zoonotic diseases' that can be passed from animals to humans are isolated, studied and genetically mutated into bio-weapons. All of this is officially denied of course (in the interests of 'plausible deniability') and the work carried out there is officially in the interests of public health. These diseases experimented with include the deadly Ebola virus, plus West Nile and Lyme disease. These are all extremely deadly and highly contagious in their own right (especially Ebola, which can cause catastrophic haemorrhaging and failure of the major organs) and by the time the research centre was finished with them are ideal agents for use in biological warfare.

However the use of animals as test subjects is one thing, but obviously human beings would be even better since in many cases the toxins developed in these facilities were specifically designed for use against humans. While there are the obvious sources of test subjects like volunteers from the armed services, something that is analogous to the civilians who are paid to take part in commercial drug trials or criminals who participate in exchange for jail privileges, there are other mean of obtaining test subjects. One such source was, rather worryingly, the Seventh-Day Adventist Church who, during the early 1950's supplied members as test subjects. They were conscientious objectors who offered to be exposed to unknown risks in return for exemption from military service.

In addition to these 'volunteers' the US (in line with other governments) has form in using other test methods, e.g. in 1966 the US military was complicit in the use of a small modified 'light bulb' filled with what was supposedly a harmless powdered stimulant, Bacillus globigii or BG, in the New York subway. The light bulbs were easy to carry and easy to break and the idea was to measure and evaluate how effectively harmful substances would spread in such an enclosed environment. Those conducting the experiment carried camouflaged, battery operated samplers to extract the air and trap the substance under test in special filters.

As it happened the subway proved to be an ideal location since each passing train created its own natural vortex and subsequent aerosol. However, it also transpired that the 'harmless stimulant' proved harmful to individuals whose immune system was either not functioning properly or who were already ill. What occurred in the New York underground system was a prophetic precursor to what actually happened in 1995, when an extremist,doomsday religious group/cult called Aum Shinrikyo released Sarin gas in the Tokyo subway system. In this attack it is estimated that around 5,000 people were affected.

Another experiment carried out on serving military personnel was 'Project Shad', this was a Navy exercise conducted under the auspices of the US Department of Defence (DoD) to find out how ships and their crews would be affected by chemical and/or biological warfare and still remain effective. Out of 134 planned tests only 46 were actually conducted and over 4,000 sailors were involved and the substances involved were Tabun, Sarin, VX nerve gas and Soman. Others were the previously mentioned Bacillus globigii, plus Coxiella burnetti and Francisella tularensis (which causes Tularemia or 'rabbit fever'). Of those who were exposed only 600 were actually informed that these experiments had ever taken place. Sadly and incredibly it seems as if, in certain circumstances using the exemptions in Public Law 105-85-NOV. 18, 1997, the US military can conduct experiments such as these on unsuspecting people.

Plum Island carries a BSL-4 (Bio-Safety Level 4) level of isolation, the other only comparable locations in the USA are the overtly military Fort Detrick in Maryland and the Centre for Disease Control and Prevention located in Atlanta. The popular TV series, 'The Walking Dead' featured this facility in one of the pivotal episodes; art imitating life perhaps, because we have no real idea of what goes on behind its walls other than what the government cares to acknowledge and even then is the information accurate or even true? Perhaps tellingly, the Plum Island facility is now administered by the secretive Department of Homeland Security.

In recent years the work at Plum Island has taken some worrying turns and twists and in 2001 there was a report in the New York Times that the US Department of Defence instigated 'Project Jefferson' in an effort at developing a new form of anthrax that was totally resistant to any known vaccine. When asked under the US FOIA (Freedom of Information Act), the Pentagon grudgingly admitted that the project did exist and would run to completion and (unsurprisingly) the results would be classified. How experiments like these can be justified tends to cast a deeply worrying shadow on the ethics and morality of those, in all nations, who embark on research of this kind. It is almost as it they want to see the ultimate doomsday weapon devised, something that is in its own way even more heinous that the devastation of thermonuclear warfare. It has been alleged by the Cuban government that in the 1960's bio-weapons developed at Plum Island were employed against it by the US in operations designed to affect its sources of revenue, like sugar cane, tobacco and pork.

Unsurprisingly, those employed at the centre do not actually live on the island, but take daily commutes from their homes in Long Island and Connecticut; this is extremely worrying because, despite the no doubt stringent isolation controls in place, the chances for infection are still there and what occurred at Gruinard Island is a case in point. In fact, mirroring what occurred there in the 1940's, during the late 1970's there were unexplained outbreaks of West Nile virus in New York City and Long Island: however these are the risks that must be taken into account when countries start conducting research on weapons such as these.

While on the subject of the staff at Plum Island, in the early days this facility like the fledgling days of NASA was reputedly staffed by scientists 'liberated' from Nazi Germany under the terms of the already mentioned US scheme 'Project Paperclip'. There is little doubt that the Nazi war machine would have benefited greatly from the horrendous experiments they carried out in the concentration camps etc. It was in these camps that the initial attempts were made at gene splicing plus some truly diabolical experiments trying to keep human organs alive while either removed from the original body, or grafted onto a foreign host. I suppose military thinking, especially when national interests are involved, can make some extremely nasty decisions using the always convenient justification of pragmatism.

The current research in the West was undoubtedly instigated by work conducted in Russia in the early 1990's when news emerged from that country stating that scientists there had successfully combined genes from a bacillus virus into anthrax thus creating a completely new and deadly hybrid. Perhaps we should pause here to consider that nature is also very adept at doing this, because new variants on the influenza virus appear almost every year, and taken at face value human beings have no part in this. Well, as far as we know, but given what all governments are capable of we should be surprised at nothing. If it is no surprise that we should be interested in what occurs in these clandestine establishments, then it follows that other eyes also follow these developments with keen interest, because there are reports of alleged UFO activity at these sites. In the 1980' and 90's several reports emerged of 'strange lights'; being seen over Plum Island and also of odd looking creatures being washed up on the neighbouring beaches. These were categorised (where this was even possible given that many of the sightings were unconfirmed) as possible ET related debris, although wiser heads attributed them directly to what was going on in the facilities on the island.

However, when looking at reports of this kind one has to keep several things in mind, not least the likelihood of mutations being accidentally introduced into the area surrounding these installations and the possibility that some of these mutations might mutate even further and travel to areas far removed from their point of origin. This would of course greatly depend on what they had been purposely designed to do, i.e. possessing speed, mobility, the ability to use their surroundings to hide and aggression. It is likely that the sightings made in the early 20th century were indeed of animals badly mutated in the very early days of gene manipulation (before it even had that name).

No system is perfect and it is possible that a few of whatever was created in these laboratories did manage to escape, either through carelessness, or even through the active collusion of people working in them. Given that they were hybrids it is also likely that they had no effective immune system and died relatively quickly once outside the labs that were their sanitised environment…either that or they were rounded up…or simply killed. Given the descriptions and locations of most of the sightings these were probably the poor creatures that were seen.

Unit 731

Would governments do this? Again unfortunately the answer is yes, they would and there is ample historical evidence to substantiate this statement. We have already seen what was done in the name of 'science' in the Nazi concentration camps, but if it is possible, these almost pale into insignificance when compared with the brutal and sadistic outrages conducted under the direct supervision of Lt General Shiro Ishii of the Imperial Japanese Army at the notorious Unit 731 situated at the Pingfang district of Harbin, the largest city in what is now Northeast China. The victims here were mainly Chinese with a percentage of Soviet and American prisoners added to provide genetic diversity, another example of grisly pragmatism.

The experiments involved vivisection, crude limb transplants, germ warfare, the effects on the body of various conventional weapons, starvation, dehydration, extremes of temperature, and being confined in high and low pressure chambers and centrifuges until dead. Again, many of the scientists involved in these truly unspeakable experiments were appropriated by the US military for its own ends in the aforementioned Project Paperclip and also simply because it prevented the Russians getting access to their knowledge. One of the men who helped run and supervise what went on there, Ryoichi Naito, a Lt Lieutenant Colonel and surgeon, went on to found one of Japan's leading pharmaceutical companies, Green Cross. It took the Japanese authorities more than fifty years to admit the horrific truth about just what occurred at this literal 'Hell on earth' and, sadly, experimentation on human beings still continues to this day in isolated absolute dictatorships like North Korea.

The Chimeras

There is no doubt that human/animal experiments are still attempted worldwide as well in various laboratories and have resulted in the deliberate production of ape/human embryos, in other words 'chimeras'. Might this be the solution regarding what is sometimes seen around these locations? At its most basic the chimera in a human form is a person of either sex who has more than one set of DNA. This condition is more common than it might appear and can occur through a quirk of nature or the deliberate manipulation of cells and it is the second of these possibilities that causes the real concern.

There have been a few acknowledged occurrences where 'natural' chimeras have been acknowledged by the medical profession. One in 1953 involved a woman in the UK who had two different blood types in her body; evidently during the conception process she had inherited blood from her twin brother and later studies indicate that this is not a rare occurrence. Another incidence of apparently spontaneous chimerism occurred in 1998 and was of a male who had some partly developed female organs; his conception was the result of in-vitro fertilisation, although whether or not this had anything to do with it is open to question.

Other instances also occurred in 2002 where, after DNA tests were conducted, it was found that the natural children belonging to a woman were genetically not hers. This came about because the woman, Lydia Fairchild, who separated from her partner while pregnant and applied for benefits, was made to undergo a DNA test to establish her relationship and the amazing outcome was the result. The courts refused to accept she was the mother and began legal proceedings, when her third child was born it was found that it was not genetically hers either. The authorities then found that her children were genetically linked to her brothers and husband and were at loss as to how to proceed. Eventually, after other tests on her skin and hair had failed to establish a link, matching DNA was found in her thyroid gland. What this also shows is that the faith of modern forensics (and the courts) in DNA based evidence has its own problems and limitations.

Some of the most worrying developments to surface are, once again, the ones that had actually appeared *and not those still secreted away in laboratories*; (my italics) of those chimeras that have been deliberately produced and admitted to. In 2003 in China at Shanghai Second Medical University researchers reported that they had finally succeeded in combining human skin cells with dead rabbit eggs and created the very first (or first openly admitted to) human chimeric embryos. The embryos were allowed to develop for several days in the laboratory then destroyed to harvest the resulting stem cells. A few years later in 2007 at the University of Nevada, scientists at the School of Medicine, in a kind of spin-off from the cloning work carried out at the Rosslyn Institute near Edinburgh, Scotland, that produced the world's first acknowledged viable clone, Dolly the sheep, created a sheep whose blood contained 15% human cells and 85% sheep cells.

Another series of experiments authorised in the UK came under the terms of the 2008 Human Fertilization and Embryology Act. The end result of these experiments, which were conducted at Kings College London, Newcastle University and Warwick University produced two different types of hybrid. One is called a chimera and the other a cybrid. Chimeras are human cells mixed with animal embryos and cybrids are created from a human nucleus being implanted into an animal cell. The experiments were eventually halted apparently due to a lack of funding, but they had resulted in the development of 155 confirmed hybrids. These were (again presumably) destroyed after the experiments were brought to a halt, but as with all reports such as these one can never be sure, especially if these hybrids were viable and there was sufficient interest from other non-academic agencies with the facilities, time, inclination, the necessary expertise and of course the money to fund further development.

Scientists have altruistically claimed that stem cells extracted from the hybrids like these could ultimately be used to treat a number of incurable diseases, but of course altruism is not always a widespread commodity, especially when there is a great deal of money to be made or some other (usual military) advantage is possible. Unsurprisingly, the implications for this kind of research are immense for all sorts of reasons, both for the drug companies and their shareholders and those in the less scrupulous world of defence, and it is much more commonplace than it used to be. Remember once again that this is the work that has so far emerged into the public domain, but there is so much more that has never, and most likely will, never be admitted to.

This includes the unfortunate creatures that may have escaped from the laboratories secreted away by various governments and fleetingly seen by members of the public. Perhaps the poor deformed creature seen at Vargina, Brazil in 1998 was such a sighting? The Vargina Case as it is called, involved what was claimed to be some kind of wounded extraterrestrial creature that was captured by the military and civilian authorities and taken away to an army base for treatment, after that nothing more is known. Yes, it might have been an extraterrestrial, but then again it might equally have been a chimera and from the description and images that are available this could well be what it was, although what it was originally created from is anyone's guess.

Folklore

Many of the fantastic creatures of folklore are chimeras and are the result of some mythological and probably magickal process. What's more, these creatures crop up repeatedly in various cultures, e.g. Egyptian (the Sphinx), Greek (Centaurs) and Persian and Japanese folklore is full of such creatures. However given the current level of research in fertility, genetics and stem cells etc. by the laboratories owned, not just by the multinational drug companies, but the deep black world of military and related sciences, literally anything is possible. Again we must confront the simple but unpalatable truth that the researchers and scientists involved in these programmes are given a more or less free hand to attempt anything.

It cannot be over emphasised that once in the world of black projects and military science tied to the intelligence community just about anything is possible and the paranoia of those involved in this dark world knows no bounds. The stories and accusations of government assassins are always totally denied, especially in the West, but there can be no doubt that they can and do happen; it is how many of these secrets are kept decades after the original programmes were closed down, because the possible reaction of the media and the public to the news of what went on is incalculable. The scientists involved in many of these projects really are in fear of their lives because of what they saw or heard, they were told to forget it; permanently. I suppose this outcome is better than what happened to the scientists employed by the Nazis at the close of WWII (those that were not swept up in Paperclip), who were simply murdered simply to ensure that no-one else benefited from their expertise and knowledge.

Much of the above comes down to the question; what is paranormal and indeed what is normal? As with most things it all depends on personal inclinations and interpretation, but the generally accepted definition of 'paranormal' is something that exists in parallel with the conventionally normal, but does not conform to that template. This description can justifiably be applied to the strange and unlikely results of the experiments conducted hidden away from prying eyes in the various top secret facilities dotted all over the world The truth of the matter is that we can never, and most likely will never, know except in some watered down and sanitised version of the truth. While it is obviously speculative, the creatures seen by the public may have been the early examples of chimeric hybrids rather than anything extraterrestrial and it would make more sense if they were, because the time scales are very similar.

As for the UFO's also allegedly seen at these establishments, it is also possible that these have been spy drones of some kind looking for evidence and their existence is both undeniable and persistent. The existence of genuine ET spacecraft can obviously never be entirely ruled out, modern UFO sightings at similar sites (as recently as 2012 for example) may also be attributable to small, almost silent stealth drones because the public has no real idea just what is still in development, the previously mentioned Hughes helicopter was the first of its kind and extremely effective too.

We should remember that what is seen in the skies at present has been in top secret development for at least twenty years or more, so what is still to come? The 'creatures' both seen at these locations and other isolated areas, well we have looked at this; specially bred chimeras and other hybrids created for surveillance and spying purposes? Why not; plausible deniability writ large? Perhaps the truth will eventually emerge and perhaps not, but in the meantime we can keep looking.

Postscript: Non-lethal Weapons

As a post script to the subject of highly sensitive and potential dangerous weapons based research carried out well away from the public's gaze, there are other equally risky and insidious projects that have been pursued in the name of defence; which involve projects falling under the general and often misleading heading of 'non-lethal technology'. This endeavour has taken many forms, including everything from 'sticky foam' that supposedly incapacitates aggressors by literally gluing them to the spot, to the use of sound frequencies that are claimed to stop aggressors in their tracks by disorienting and otherwise incapacitating them.

As part of this technology, one of the avenues of research attempted involved so-called 'psycho-corrective devices' and how they could be used effectively both in warfare and as measures in civilian crowd control. The idea behind these devices was that commands and instructions could be implanted in the human brain subconsciously via specific frequencies without disrupting the main intellectual and neurological processes needed for the individual to function. In other words the subject would experience a sudden impulse to take a specific course of action (i.e. to lie down and stop shooting, or fall asleep, or turn round and walk away, or some other action that would inhibit their role) simply because it seems like a better course of action.

This was supposed to be used to control riots and demoralise or destabilise opponents and was begun by the work of Dr. Ross Adey (amongst others) who discovered that behaviour can be directly affected by placing a subject in an electromagnetic field. This seems to fit nicely with the research of Prof Michael Persinger who has produced similar effects in subjects by subjecting them to various magnetic fields. In this case it produced the impression of a presence and that someone was with them even although the subject (all volunteers it should be stressed) knew no one was there.

Projects have included: Sleeping Beauty, whose purpose should be self-evident and Project Monarch, which is designed to quickly induce severe and incapacitating personality disorders. Similar technologies were supposedly employed by the FBI at the notorious siege involving David Koresh, (aka Vernon Howell) and the Branch Davidians at Waco in Texas, although this is hotly disputed. It is known that, in common with techniques used during the siege of General Manuel Noriega, the compound was bombarded day and night by very loud music to ostensibly disorientate the occupants. However it is thought that this music acted as both a screen and a carrier for other, more subtle frequencies. Another weapon deployed used extremely bright, low frequency strobe lights: a far cry indeed from the relatively primitive, but highly effective (and aptly named) 'brown noise', which was specifically designed to make the person affected by it lose the will to fight by spontaneously voiding their bowels.

Another location where this technology, this time using microwaves, is thought to have been used is at a former RAF facility at Greenham Common, the scene of considerable peaceful lobbing by protestors against the storage of cruise missiles at the USAF base which had been there since 1943. The Greenham Common peace camp was opened in 1982 and continued, remarkably enough, until 2000 when the last of the protestors finally left. This was despite the fact that the last of the missiles were removed in 1991 following the Intermediate-Range Nuclear Forces Treaty. It is thought that the camp still served a useful purpose by supplying a rallying point for various dissident groups and reminding the public of the dangers of harbouring nuclear weapons.

Uncomfortable and unpalatable as it might be, sadly it can be no other way and the aims of the pacifists, although entirely laudable only succeed in a perfect world where everyone plays both fairly and by the same set of rules. Regrettably the world we live in is not like that and we see this every single day, so all that would happen is that we would ultimately be delivered into the hands and whims of our enemies. Whether these enemies are extraterrestrial or located solidly here on Earth in the end makes little difference, because without the various agencies conducting these unpalatable measures on our behalf what would happen? Perhaps this is best summed up in the words of the late visionary and prophetic writer George Orwell when he said, '*We sleep safely in our beds because rough men stand ready in the night to do evil in our name*'.

Chapter Four
Dissonance and the True Believer

Just before the millennium occurred amid much fanfare, I wrote a magazine article called 'The End of Days…Daze', which pondered on the more obvious and blatant End Times nonsense, the more outrageous the better, how it was promoted and why it was eagerly snapped up and accepted as fact by various groups of what one can only refer to as 'true believers'. I wondered why, what was the attraction? A bit of research revealed that there seems to be a good reason for it. Why do you suppose that a disparate group of people who band together under whatever belief system, be it Ufological, religious or perhaps a cult (although you could argue that they are all part and parcel of the same thing) become convinced that they are correct even when they are repeatedly proven wrong?

Before looking at the rationale and logic behind this phenomenon we should first look at a few groups that fall precisely within this category. One of the most widely held example of this comes from the teachings of the Jehovah's Witnesses (which has also sometimes been referred to as a cult) who are convinced that come the End Times only 144,000 souls will be saved and taken to Heaven. The say this is because of what is written in the Book of Revelations 7:1-8 and 14:1-5, which says basically that 12,000 people will be drawn from each of the twelve tribes of Israel, they will be the chosen people and they are all Jehovah's Witnesses.

The rest of us, that's you and me, are doomed! None of this takes into account that the Book of Revelations was a blatant propaganda exercise written by someone with a very clear agenda who was determined to terrify unbelievers into accepting their version of scripture. It has been used to justify all sorts of bizarre beliefs, including dire warnings about the imminent world takeover and domination by New World Order. To be fair though this sort of extreme and literalist belief is true of adherents of all religious books irrespective of the faith.

Overtly religious groups aside and there are quite a few of various hues and flavours, one of the prime contenders that absolutely typify this mindset originated in the tidal wave of UFO groups that began in the late 1940's early 1950's. They were originally called *'The Seekers'*, but later adopted the title (and this is **much** more impressive) *'The Brotherhood of the Seven Rays'*. With a name like that it is likely that they attracted a wide range of members with a latent pseudo-mystical/quasi-religious bent. The group was founded in 1954 by a Chicago housewife, Mrs Dorothy Martin; although clearly aware of her own divinity she quickly adopted the name, 'Sister Thedra'.

Given her self-appointed mission this title better suited her views of both her abilities and place in the great scheme of things. She was what is commonly referred to as a 'channeller' and probably significantly had previously been involved with Ron Hubbard's system of Dianetics, which was and still is a technique developed by Hubbard to supposedly promote mental health. It should be stressed that this is not necessarily directly connected to Scientology, a system of belief also developed by Ron Hubbard, although it obviously has many close similarities. Given Dorothy Martin/Sister Thedra's background it is scarcely surprising that her group incorporated many of the techniques which later emerged in the Scientology movement.

Sister Thedra was considered blessed by her followers, mainly because she had (largely by her own admission) been chosen to receive messages via a mediumistic system called 'automatic writing'. This involves the person (who is invariably also a medium or a channeller; although for all practical purposes there is little or no difference) falling into a light trance and allowing themselves to become possessed by an external intelligence. The 'intelligence' then conveys its message via a pen or pencil which is held in the hand of the channellers', onto a piece of paper. This form of communication is potentially risky and seems rather at odds with traditional teaching about such matters where possession is to be avoided at all costs because of the possible negative fallout, which can be both emotionally and physically draining to the point of causing real harm to the person who is apparently possessed.

Trance and physical mediums (there are several kinds who work differently) do this on a regular basis when they allow their regular 'spirit guide', or sometimes any passing spirit, to temporarily take over their body and use it to permit communication. In the case of physical mediums the change is often marked with very real alterations seeming to take place to the appearance of the body and face of the medium. Therefore it rather depends on what is doing the possessing, because some of the entities in the spirit realm are not necessarily what they claim to be; so one can only assume (or hope) that when voluntary possession occurs it is safe, at least for the human partner.

At any rate Sister Thedra conveyed a series of apocalyptic messages from altruistic aliens on the distant planet Clarion prophesying the imminent inundation of planet Earth by floods (evidently the first biblical attempt was not enough). This is a curious and borderline illogical concept, since to inundate the entire planet there would have to be more water on it than is already there in the first place. The only way that might occur would be through sudden and catastrophic global warming causing the polar ice caps to melt, something that was not even considered when Sister Thedra was conveying her doom-laden messages. There was even a date set: the early hours of the 21st of December 1954, very precise and typical of others (and as with overtly religious prophecies there have been many) who have predicted other versions of the End Times.

She must have touched a nerve in some sections of the populace; (although there is always a ready market for this kind of outré prophecy), and she attracted many devotees. The general idea was as with many similar groups, Marshall Applewhite's 'Heavens Gate' was another but considerably more tragic example, that the chosen few will be swept up in a flying saucer and taken to the home planet of their erstwhile saviours and as we will soon see there are still variants on this belief system around today. Such was their level of certainty of those who flocked to Sister Thedra that, displaying another trait common in prophesies like these, they abandoned secure jobs, left their wives and/or husbands and gave away their possessions in the knowledge that they would be saved. In the cases of the tragic Heavens Gate devotees, their spacecraft was supposed to be hidden in the tail of the rather spectacular comet 'Hale Bop'.

According to the channelled messages, just before midnight on the 20th of December a representative from Clarion would arrive at the house and lead the believers to the warm sanctuary of a spacecraft that would be conveniently parked nearby for boarding. However the representative did not appear and when the appointed time, 4am, came and went and there was still no sign of the promised courier quite understandably the group was stunned and Sister Thedra began to weep and lament: but a solution soon followed. At around 5pm another channelled message was received by the still weeping Sister Thedra; God had decided to spare the Earth from destruction because this little group had kept the faith and, quote, *'spread so much light that He had saved the world from destruction'*; no doubt much jubilation and joy ensued. Hopefully this was adequate compensation for those who had given away or otherwise disposed of all their worldly goods.

There are many other examples of this, although with no corresponding predictions of destruction, too many to detail here, but here are a few, 'The Industrial Church of The New World Comforter' is one example. 'The Industrial Church of The New World Comforter' was the 1973 invention of Allen Michael in response to telepathic contact with UFOs. Michael was formerly known by the more prosaic surname of Noonan, but decided that Michael chimed more with the titular Archangel, and had experienced at least two previous UFO contacts; one in 1947 (again that amazingly prophetic year) and another in 1954 at Giant Rock, which stands seven stories high, in the Mojave Desert.

It should come as no surprise to learn that the rock stands on ground once leased by another UFO contactee George van Tassel and has been the site of several UFO conferences. Michael also released his vision of salvation in a book entitled *'The Everlasting Gospel'*, which became the standard bible of his group, now styling itself as 'The One World Family'. We should bear in mind the almost seismic changes occurring during this period of the 1960's when the New Age had begun to take root and groups such as this sprang up like the macrobiotic food (including hallucinogenic mushrooms) that they consumed.

These groups are lightweights compared to the 'E-Bible Fellowship' from the United States who loudly proclaim that Jesus Christ, presaged by violent earthquakes and great calamity, would return in all his glory on May the 21th 2011. It might be churlish to suggest that this group were obviously trying to upstage other End Times proponents who put the date a little later at the 23rd of December 2012. This group run by Chris McCann and the 89 year old Harold Camping, both avid Christian evangelical fundamentalists, insist that Jesus disowned churches and all they stood for in 1988 and when He returns it's no good heading to the nearest church for salvation because anyone who does is too late and automatically doomed.

They base this alarming prediction on their own highly individual interpretation of the bible and Pastor Camping goes a far as to say, *"Beyond the shadow of a doubt, May 21 will be the date of the Rapture and the day of judgment,"* Rather more enigmatically, in answer to those who pooh-pooh this idea as one among many End Time prophecies, the equally certain Chris McCann says that, *"It would be like telling the Wright brothers that every other attempt to fly has failed, so you shouldn't even try,"* It has to be said that other fringe religious group are also joining in the general furor about it and adding their collective voices to that of Pastor Camping in awaiting His return. 2008 had also been claimed as the beginning of the end when the first trumpet sounded with the crash of the US economy and the corresponding worldwide meltdown of financial markets. Strange is it not that money, the root of all evil, is seen as the precursor to the apocalypse, but then again this all starts with cynical affront of American evangelical and Pentecostal 'prosperity ministries'.

It is groups like the E-bible Fellowship and their literalist fellow travellers who accept the Bible as the literal, revealed word of God rather than the mixture of history, allegory, metaphor, magick, gnosis and fable that it actually is. Unlikely as it might seem these believers are absolutely convinced that the idea of physical levitation as in The Rapture is a given and when the End Times come and the Antichrist emerges, they, and they alone, will be raised up into the air to remain in safety while the rest of humanity suffers in what they call 'The Tribulation'. The number designated for salvation is, as mentioned at the start of this chapter, remarkably specific at 144,000.

They are always remarkably good at defining precisely who, when and what will occur
They base their Rapture beliefs on the following biblical prophesy: Thessalonians 4:16-17 says, *'And the dead in Christ will rise first: then we who are alive, who are left, shall be caught up together with them in the clouds to meet the Lord in the air, and so we shall always be with the Lord'.* They see nothing odd or unusual about this, and actively embrace it as a received truth; in fact it draws a parallel with the Islamic belief that the faithful who die in the service of Allah will live forevermore in Allah's garden and every whim will be attended to by 70 beautiful virgins. Although one faith is rather more pragmatic and earthy than the other, they do both allude to war and strife as the backdrop of their salvation. Despite the fact that the ethos for both belief systems is one of humility and peace, they do in fact feature war and combat in their structure, i.e. *'Onward Christian soldiers marching off to war'* and of course the superstitious, bloodthirsty and pointless religious slaughter of the Crusades.

Continuing on the perverse themes of war and eventual salvation, shortly after The Tribulation comes Armageddon when the armies of Heaven battle the forces of Satan and the Antichrist on the plains of Megiddo in Israel. Once the forces of light win, and evidently this is another given that has abundantly clear supernatural and magickal overtones, and Satan is safely locked away, those who had been Raptured will return to live in a 'Heaven on earth'.

However there is still more to come and one thousand years after Armageddon, Satan escapes from capture and once again challenges the forces of light. This time the earth itself is destroyed, but a new one descends from the Heavens and at long last there is everlasting and eternal peace. After this mayhem with its precursor of mass levitations, what was the mechanism that brought it all about? Unfortunately, as with the levitating saints, the answer is 'the power of God', which needs no explanation whatsoever. All of this seems to indicate that The Bible, instead of the revealed word of Almighty God, might equally be a treatise on magick, which it is of course exactly what it is.

The same is also true when one encounters the claims of levitation exhibited by those who are in the thrall of Satanic and/or demonic forces. It is a fairly standard ploy used in cinematic representations of demonic possession where the individual who is possessed is levitated into the air then set back down again. Logic suggests that the mechanism must be the same, but one is approved (i.e. the power of God) and the other is not, (the power of Satan). In both cases what is demonstrated is clearly an example of magick, but for some reason this is a word that would never be considered, although to mark the difference between the two powers anything purporting to come from God might be referred to as 'white magick' and from Satan as 'black magick'.

The same is true in such influential fictional literary works as the 'Lord of The Rings' trilogy where there is a 'white wizard', Gandalf, and his evil (ergo 'black wizard') counterpart Sauron. The similarities between the Gandalf/Christ, Sauron/Satan imagery are also striking in that in his efforts to protect his flock he is initially killed by the forces of Sauron, but later returns in all his glory to vanquish the might of the dark empire. It is also notable that the forces of evil are portrayed as uniformly hideous and unspeakably brutal. On the other hand those under the protection of Gandalf are seen as naïve, loyal, kindly and well meaning and backed up by elemental forces that for the most part are either semi or wholly magickal.

Neither is it an accident that the name, Sauron, is chosen because of its obvious connection to the world of reptiles (Saurians) and indeed Satan is often referred to as 'that old dragon'. In spite of these loaded semantic considerations the only place that hard parallels like this can be made is in the world of allegory and fiction, because with breathtaking hypocrisy representatives of all the mainstream religions balk at the very thought that miracles, because of negative associations, could possibly be defined as magick.

Returning to UFO centred belief, there is a third order of phenomena which is rarely mentioned in this context and that is what supposedly happens during alien abduction scenarios when the abductee is 'levitated' into, presumably non-terrestrial spacecraft. This gives rise to serious consideration of alleged levitations attributed to saints and other assorted holy people and the claims made about the Rapture. This particular area tends to blur the boundaries between religion, magick and some of the more left field versions of Ufology where the believers are sure that levitation and the Rapture are a misinterpretation of their own technology based paradigm. These particular believers are sure that prior to 'the end' the human race will indeed be lifted up in its entirety (and not just a chosen few) from the face of the Earth, but in a fleet of giant spacecraft.

These spacecraft are evidently already here on permanent standby and are currently parked in orbit around the moon, but they are 'cloaked' and therefore invisible. In this version of the myth, rather than the forces of darkness, viz. Satan and the Antichrist ranged against those of light, viz. Christ, there are two races of extraterrestrials fighting over the earth and its population. This is a hypothesis that, when one looks at it, runs parallel to accepted wisdom; the only differences are in the context and the end results are of course rather different. This version of events has the friendly ET's (blond, tall, blue eyed 'Nordics', a clear parallel with angels) in combat with the non-friendly ET's (nasty, reptilian beings, the comparison with demons is not difficult to make) over the fate of humanity. However, humanity is conveniently well out of the way aboard these truly gigantic spacecraft and the outcome is a forgone conclusion. The 'good' ET's defeat the 'bad' ET's and humanity either returns to the earth or travels with the 'good' ET's to their idyllic home worlds (Heaven).

Rather worryingly, groups such as the notorious and poisonous *'Westboro Baptist Church'*, (membership around 100) which labours along under the spiteful rhetoric of Pastor Fred Phelps, who describes himself as a 'primitive Baptist', hitches its scruffy dogma to the apocalyptic visions of the E-Bible Fellowship. Not only that, but a similarly narrow minded and vicious outfit calling itself *'The Rapture Right'* has likewise decided that the end is nigh and only they will be saved. They won't of course, because the End Times are not coming any time soon unless the human race brings it about through its own stupidity. They are wrong, and they will be proven wrong, but they will still keep plodding on even more determined than before, why? It is an example of what was mentioned at the beginning of the book, it is called 'cognitive dissonance'.

This is a state of mind where one person, or a group of people, simultaneously maintains two competing and diametrically opposed opinions leading to absolute turmoil in their thought processes. To avoid this, as in the case of Sister Thedra and her cosy 'Brotherhood of the Seven Rays', when the prophecy dramatically failed she deflected it by channelling the message that all was well because God had stopped it happening. She could also have simply provided another date, but that too would have failed to materialise, so the best thing was to call the whole thing off. It should be noted that all of the followers had invested heavily in the prophecy by selling up their properties etc. so they could not afford to have the prophecy obviously fail; after all how foolish would they look never mind their impending penury? The other way around this is to recruit as many like minded individuals as possible to reinforce their belief, after all if they all think the same then it can't be wrong...right? Wrong!

An identical effect is seen when faith healers claim to heal the sick by supposedly using the power of God to heal, it does not matter what the illness is, cancer, MS, Parkinson's or whatever, God will heal it. The relief felt by the sufferer is almost always psychosomatic and transient in nature, but that does not matter because it's a 'miracle'. When the condition manifests again, and it will, then the sufferer simply did not have sufficient faith hence the miracle did not happen. Healers? No; shameless liars, charlatans and often thieves demanding 'donations' to carry on the 'Lord's work'. Where cures are effected (always for medical conditions, no arms or legs have ever been regrown) then perhaps the sufferer did not have any ailment in the first place, or perhaps they actually did cure themselves by some misunderstood mechanism, an example of the placebo effect perhaps and that can be remarkably effective, who knows?

Before ending there is at least one more prediction of the End Times still to come, this time from no less a visionary that great polymath Sir Isaac Newton who, using the book of Daniel, decided that the end of the world would occur in 2060. To be fair to Newton he was an extremely able and intelligent man who spent a considerable amount of time wrestling with subjects that would now fall under the general heading of cosmology if not magick. This was no mean feat considering the level of scientific understanding at that time, but we should also bear in mind that Newton based his predictions on religion rather than logic and science. However we can't really blame him for that simply because, again in Newton's era, scripture was generally held to be absolutely true and beyond reproach and besides, the great scientist was mystically inclined.

Unfortunately for the 'true believers', and there are many, none of this will ever matter and they will continue quite happily on their deluded way falling for fast-talking, snake oil salesmen promising them everything from miracle cures to forgiveness and safety from the apocalypse of the End Times that continually threatens the human race, but, somehow, never quite arrives. As long as there are conmen out there (and maybe some of them actually believe what they are preaching), there will always be a ready and willing supply of dupes ready to buy into whatever is on offer. Maybe we actually need it and it's an instinct hardwired into us, a survival mechanism of sorts, and if it is be sure that someone, somewhere, will always be ready to exploit it for their own ends.

The problem with the beliefs espoused by the 'true believers' in whatever their system of belief happens to be, is that for them their ideas can never be satisfactorily disproved or shown to be false simply because anyone who does produce valid and irrefutable evidence, be it scientist or journalist, that undermines their belief, automatically causes the 'plot' to expand to include the person providing the conflicting evidence. In other words irrespective of how good the evidence is, it must be a lie designed to undermine them and whoever provides the information becomes part of the plot. This is what drives and provides rationale to many of those espousing the outer limits of belief. The other side of the coin suggests that society has only itself to blame through the inequalities that have polarised it and created distrust and disillusionment and provided fertile ground upon which to sow many of the more bizarre ideas around today. They succeed simply because they supply certainty in troubled times.

Chapter Five
The ET Inside

Has anyone ever considered the possibility that the human race might be extraterrestrial in its own right? In fact this is more than a consideration; it is almost a certainty! This observation is based on the fact that we and every single living thing on this planet, whether animal or vegetable, is composed of DNA: so where did the DNA originate? Was it something that happened by sheer chance in, as has been speculated, one of the 'small warm pools' that dotted the surface of our planet as has been suggested by some schools of thought? Or did this event occur in the oceans as a result of electrical interaction, e.g. lightning, with clouds of random chemicals, or, as has also been suggested somewhere else entirely?

This alternative suggestion puts forward the hypothesis that DNA is no accident; it is the result of panspermia. Panspermia centres on the theory that the chemicals necessary to create life came from meteors and other celestial bodies that sometimes collide with our planet. It is widely recognised that within its virtually limitless void, the universe is absolutely packed with all the requisite components drifting around in clouds and that meteors and other small, travelling celestial bodies have traces of these materials in various combinations as part of their composition. We know this because when scientifically tested, traces of the building blocks of DNA (if not the DNA itself) have been found in many fragments of space debris that has crashed onto the surface of our planet. Among these materials are formaldehyde, methane, types of alcohol and sugars plus other organic compounds; all just floating around out in space.

The Millar-Urey Experiment

Let's first look at the possibility that life initially came about by the action of random but natural electrical processes. As far as spontaneous creation is concerned, this was attempted in the famous (some might say infamous) Millar-Urey Experiment. In 1953 a series of laboratory experiments were conducted at the University of Chicago by Stanley Miller and Harold Urey in an attempt to recreate the conditions thought to be prevalent when life first appeared on the Earth. This also was the birth of a scientific discipline called *prebiotic chemistry* and the process became known as *'The Miller-Urey Experiment'*. The concept was designed to test a hypothesis first promoted by Haldane and Oparin who suggested that, given the right conditions, inorganic components on the early Earth could be spontaneously metamorphosised into organic compounds.

Millar and Urey built an apparatus resembling two glass spheres, each about the size of a soccer ball located one on top of the other with electrodes set into the top flask and connected using tubes. The bottom sphere was half filled with a mix of water, methane, ammonia and hydrogen, which were all assumed to have been present during the formation of the planet, then heat was applied. As steam was produced through evaporation it was introduced into the top flask where the electrodes were located and electrical discharges were produced there to simulate lightening in the hope that chemical compounds would appear. The condensate in the top flask then ran back into the bottom in a continuous process. Unfortunately the experiments, although not entirely successful, did, after a week of continuous operation, produce a small amount of the amino acids necessary to manufacture proteins. Certain sugars and some of the other components of nucleic acids were also produced.

The work started by Millar and Urey has continued intermittently ever since and as recently as 2008 eleven vials left from the original experiment were re-evaluated by another team of scientists using much more effective and sensitive measuring equipment. They were able to identify additional organic molecules not previous noted by Millar and Urey and confirmed that the best results came from the original attempt to recreate 'volcano like' conditions. In spite of the lack of complete success it still does not mean that it cannot be done and significantly, the hypothesis of the 'warm pool' put forward by Darwin may have been infinitely bigger than he might originally have envisioned. Another experiment conducted in 2006 indicated that a dense organic haze, which contained various concentrations of methane and carbon dioxide, might have existed over much of the very early Earth.

These microscopic organic molecules that formed thus haze would have dispersed and proliferated naturally all over the surface of the planet bringing with them the necessary building blocks by means of convection currents, winds and other forces. It is an astonishing mental image, the entire planet completely enveloped in a mantle of fog containing the seeds of life itself, like a gigantic biochemistry set. Although the experiments first promoted in 1953 still continue, currently there are some serious questions being put forward about where we as a race go from here. Do we continue to evolve or since the creation of life has apparently not been successfully replicated either naturally or artificially since its inception, has our evolution as a species now effectively ceased?

The answer to this is at best unclear, which in turn, since the original creation of the human race as envisioned by scripture, although convenient is extremely unlikely, invites another and much more viable solution. However it is not one that sits comfortably with any paradigm so far mentioned; it is called 'Panspermia'. Before considering this perhaps we should take a look at Darwin and what his far-reaching and radical discoveries implied. Incidentally, in spite of the limited success of the experiments considered so far, the method by which chemicals become 'alive' has still not been discovered. This is strange because it happens quite naturally the world over hundreds of times each second when children are conceived. Perhaps this is what is meant by the 'miracle' of life and the effectively magickal process that makes 'dead' chemicals alive.

Although that analogy is not quite accurate since the sperm and egg are both 'alive', they still require to be merged with one another to allow sentient life to commence. Before leaving what was attempted by Millar and Urey we should also consider its direct predecessor and that was the astonishing work carried out by Andrew Crosse in 1837. It was in this year that Crosse allegedly succeeded in using the then novel medium of electrical power to create a type of life, in this case an entirely new species of insect. However, first let's briefly look at Charles Darwin and his theories about evolution and survival through natural selection.

Charles Darwin

Darwin was born in Shropshire to a wealthy family, and attended an elite private school from where he graduated to Edinburgh University to study medicine. This choice of career evidently did not suit him, so in 1827 he entered Cambridge University with the intention of becoming a clergyman in the Church of England. While studying there he met two men who were to prove pivotal in his career. They were Adam Sedgewick and John Henslow, one a geologist, the other a naturalist. From them Darwin learned the multiple skills and techniques of observation plus collecting and mounting specimens. Graduating from Cambridge in 1831 aged only twenty-two, Darwin was taken on board the English survey ship the HMS Beagle as an unpaid naturalist.

It was during this voyage that, as a result of his findings regarding the staggering complexity and variety of the creatures he studied, he was forced to confront the perceived wisdom of the era the so called 'catastrophist theory'. This, along with the bible, was the cornerstone of conventional creationist belief, i.e. that the earth, the universe and all it contained was brought about by the word of God. It postulated that the Earth had experienced a whole succession of creations, each destroyed by a sudden catastrophe. The last cataclysm had been the flood of Noah, which had wiped out all life on Earth save the animals that were on board the ark, taken there by Noah at Gods' command.

Actually if one thinks about it the flood as envisaged by creationists cannot have happened (the entire planet would have to have been inundated) and it impossible for Noah, quite apart from preserving the plant life, to have taken two of each species of every living creature on Earth aboard his Ark. All the fossils unearthed by archaeologists to date constitute the remains of those destroyed in previous disasters. In the view of the catastrophists and creationists, all species were created individually and were unchangeable for evermore. When he returned to England, Darwin set about recording his findings on changeability, which finally culminated in his 1859 seminal work 'On the Origin of Species by means of Natural Selection'. This revolutionary work literally stood convention on its head; even his later works including 'The Descent of Man' did not evoke the same outraged response.

The net result of the controversy was the creation of two distinct schools of thought; the church led 'creationists' and the sectarian 'evolutionists'. At first there was widespread condemnation from the churches and the scientific establishment, but over time there came a gradual albeit grudging acceptance of the theory. However this was not universal especially in

America where it led to court cases, most notably the famous 1926 'Scopes Monkey Trial' in Tennessee, which caught the attention and imagination of the world. Proponents of the biblical creationist tradition went to court to prevent the theory of evolution being taught in schools. The evolutionists' case was fought by the famous lawyer Clarence Darrow; he won and the rest as they say is history. Unfortunately, given the influence that religion wields in some states in the USA creationism has made a partial return. Although what Darwin demonstrated had very obvious attractions, it did not explain how life actually began, this was mainly because the techniques to do so had not been invented let alone thought of.

The Crosse Experiments

A truly fascinating precursor to the experiments made famous by Millar and Urey was the work carried out by what must surely have been one of the last of the English 'gentleman scientists'. He was a dilettante in the truest and best sense of the word and his name was Andrew Crosse, (1784-1855) and in a classic example of synchronicity Crosse carried out a series of experiments using electricity, although his original purpose was quite different. He was born to a wealthy land owning family and was regarded as something of a prodigy having managed to learn Greek by the age of eight. On reaching the age of nine he was sent for further schooling to the seaport of Bristol where he became fascinated by the new science of electricity, the possibilities of which later became an obsession with him.

When his mother died in 1805 he inherited a considerable sum of money, more than enough to support him, and also the isolated family seat of Fyne Court mansion house located in the Quantock Hills of Somerset, England. The isolated location of his home was ideal for his experiments and in order to utilise the natural power of lightning, he laid out a network of copper cables over a mile in length that radiated from his laboratory like the strands of a spiders web. The largely uneducated local population were far from knowledgeable about what he was doing and as result both distrusted and eventually feared him. They regarded his work as on a par with sorcery and the sight of lightning strikes from the thunderstorms that occasionally swirled and blustered their way around the hills arcing along the network of cables reinforced this perception and absolutely terrified them.

It has to be said that anyone, especially then, who tried to use the intermittent raw energy of lightening as a source of power was, from the point of view of safety on very thin ice indeed, and it can only be due to sheer luck that he was not killed. Since he must have been largely basing these experiments on sheer guesswork it is not at all clear how he managed to regulate the short lived, high intensity of the voltage created by the lightening to a usable level. It is possible that he may have used the initial lightening discharge to energise capacitors for a later and slower discharge, but like many of the experiments carried out during this period, especially those conducted by amateurs, this is not made clear. In the course of his experiments, which were originally intended for the unrelated purpose of producing artificial minerals from saturated solutions, he made another astonishing discovery.

His apparatus, a basic set up which comprised a cloth siphoning a drip feed of sample liquid from a top container on to a piece of porous red oxide kept electrified in a lower container, was under constant close observation by means of a magnifying glass to detect signs of spontaneous crystal growth. After fourteen days there appeared what he described as small, pallid 'excrescences' and on the eighteenth day they enlarged slightly and produced seven to eight filaments. On the twenty-sixth day each of the 'excrescences' resembled tiny insects and moved their 'legs' and a few days later they detached themselves and moved around independently, naturally Crosse was astonished and repeated the experiment *with identical results*, (my italics).

Crosse named the insects *'acari'* and once again carried out the experiments using a range of materials and still with the same results. Eventually he wrote up the results and after meeting initial scepticism from the scientific establishment, one Mr. W.H Weeks a well know scientist, was commissioned to replicate the Crosse experiments. Weeks employed even more stringent controls, including sterilisation of all the equipment, but in spite of this succeeded in producing near identical results and the tiny creatures were called *'Acarus Crossi'* in honour of their discoverer/creator. Quite naturally the religious authorities were outraged at this apparent blasphemy and the local clergyman, a Rev Philip Smith, was called in and actually exorcised Crosse's estate. The account of this discovery goes on to insist that even today no scientist is willing to attempt this remarkable experiment and one might justifiably ask why? What is there to fear?

So goes the tale which only creates many more questions than answers, it has been suggested that the small mites were already present as eggs in the atmosphere or on the samples used by both experimenters. Did Crosse perhaps bribe Weeks into corroborating his claims? He certainly had the money. Why would modern science not follow up these experiments, because this would surely prove whether (or not) there was some basis in fact for the claims made by Crosse and Weeks? It cannot be due to fear of religious wrath, for if it were proved correct then surely this would be a major discovery? One thing that does strike a sympathetic chord are the extremely caustic conditions in which these 'acari' appeared, they developed in a hostile environment analogous to the conditions that supposedly brought about our own templates for life.

The story of Crosse and his experiments carry more than a little of the feel of the story of Frankenstein; the purpose was the same, the details are all there even down to the superstitious reactions of the villagers surrounding his estates. It also resonates strongly with the same use of lightning that Mary Shelley's envisioned for the motivating power behind Baron Victor Frankenstein's experiments. Is it possible that she knew of what Crosse did and used it as a framework for her own creation? Based on that premise it is almost impossible to separate the gothic images created by Shelly and later in the cinema with what went on at Fyne Court. But still the doubt persists: in spite of claims to the contrary were these insects spontaneously created by no more than the action of electricity on specific chemicals, or is this just one more semi-scientific hoax perpetrated on a gullible society, another example of disinformation carried on into modern times by theorists with their own unknown agenda? One thing that does ring true is that the scientific descendents of Crosse did succeed in reproducing at least some of the steps required to replicate the process of life…but why the apparent failure of modern science to replicate what Crosse did? If the results attained by Crosse were successfully replicated by at least one of his peers, why nothing since?

Directed Panspermia

There is however yet another possibility and although related to panspermia it is much more focussed, it is called 'directed panspermia' and suggests that life here on Earth was not a random act, but was brought about deliberately by a being or beings unknown for purposes that are equally unknown. Therefore if that is feasible then we can consider the deliberate and calculated seeding of our planet using, let's call them *'life packets'*. This has obvious attractions, but as with many revolutionary ideas it also introduces a number of other questions, like why this particular planet? Is it because of the so-called 'Goldilocks Zone' i.e. the planetary position of the Earth in relation to the Sun; not too hot, not too cold, just enough oxygen, the right level of gravity, just enough water etc, etc?

Bear in mind that all this would have occurred *after* a prolonged 'settling in' process. The concept of directed panspermia came from such luminaries as Sir Francis Crick (one of the discoverers of DNA) and an astronomer the late Sir Fred Hoyle. This concept resonates well with the idea of exogenesis, or that life originated not on the earth but elsewhere. Crick promoted this idea because he was convinced that, due to its astonishing complexity, the formation of DNA could not have been an accident. He did later modify his views to those shared by evolutionists, i.e. that it did develop by natural methods, but with some important questions (unfortunately) left unanswered. Not least of these is one we have already encountered, 'abiogenesis', or the reason and mechanism by which life originated from non-living components.

In fact if one considers it then how do the individual chemicals and components of sperm and egg *on their own* become 'alive' when combined? It seems therefore that much of the hard work was already done to allow sentient life to develop on the Earth. It is as well to make clear that the process of abiogenesis is not the same as spontaneous creation (with which it is sometimes confused). The process of abiogenesis took place over millions of years, whereas spontaneous creation means just that, viz, that life appeared in an instant. Originally spontaneous creation held considerable sway and was supposedly 'proven' to exist by various scientists including Jan Baptist van Helmont (1580–1644), who produced a formula for creating mice.

This unlikely process involved a piece of soiled cloth wrapped around some wheat and left for 21 days; then scorpions and basil, (placed between two bricks and left in sunlight) were added. All of this seems laughable now, but bear in mind that other individuals suggested equally unlikely things while working as alchemists. Another belief i.e. that rotting meat spontaneously gave birth to maggots, was proven wrong in 1668, when Francesco Redi noted that meat sealed in containers did not produce maggots. So he covered some meat with fine cloth and let nature take its course. When the meat eventually became rotten he noted that there were maggots on the cloth, but not the meat, and from that deduced that it was flies (attracted by the stench) laying eggs that caused the maggots to appear. It was due to experiments such as these that the theory of spontaneous creation was quashed.

However with panspermia, if this was how life arrived on earth it is much more likely that a large number of 'life packets' were dispatched more or less at random to land where they would and, if the conditions were righ̄ develop. Does this infer that the creation of the solar system and its planets and even the 'Late Heavy Bombardment' (LHB) was actually a precursor to the seeding process? The LHB is assumed to have occurred around 3.2 billion years ago, shortly after the Earth's crust formed in fact, although the word 'shortly' in geological terms is entirely relative since the solar system itself is around 5 billion years old and the universe in the order of 14.2 billion.

The LHB consisted of thousands of large meteors and asteroids originating from the edges of the solar system when it became unstable due to changes in the position of Jupiter and Saturn, raining down upon the surface of the Earth. Well, that's one theory, but at least it is supported by geological discoveries made on the moon, where the abundant and massive cratering shows signs of such an event occurring and if it happened to the moon then it probably happened to the Earth (and the other planets) too. That being the case, the planet's surface would have been completely and permanently changed, almost back to the original molten state of the 'Hadean Age' when the Earth was still forming.

This tends to rule out the possibility that the components of DNA arrived via that manner *at that time* since the destruction would have been almost absolute and nothing could have survived, so the process must have begun when conditions were much more amenable. It has even been suggested quite reasonably that life on earth came from the planet Mars, although whether this was in the form of 'life packets' is another matter entirely. By the same token it has been suggested that the planet Earth has itself been responsible for sending it's own chemicals into space via the mechanism of ejected solids being thrown up when struck by meteors, perhaps the LHB was a two way street? If directed panspermia is feasible, this assumes that the 'life packets' were more or less uniform and contained the same or similar ingredients, which in this case may imply that all life in the universe must be basically the same. The other alternative is that the 'life packets' contained a range of building blocks suitable for a wide range of conditions. In other words, irrespective of where the 'packets' arrived they contained the raw material to create life, where life, *any form of life*, was possible.

It is this point of transition of non-life to life that produces the really difficult question and the main bone of contention between the rabid rationalists who choose to believe (based on their interpretation of the evidence) that we are the products of a still ongoing series of amazing and happy accidents and other equally qualified people who see things rather differently. This is not to say that those who do not accept that life is no more than series of accidents believe that some magickal figure created the universe by an act of will alone, but that there was some kind of causal principle guiding the process along. In other words this was not simply due to an unfathomable and unknowable divine act from God.

This of course raises all sorts of fascinating questions that apply to all life in the universe and not just the human race, because surely God (assuming that there is one) did not just create the human race to exist all on its own in the mind numbing enormity of the universe. That is genuinely worrying, all on our own in the universe, surely not? What happens if (or when) we finally either poison ourselves or overpopulate ourselves to extinction, because neither of the possibilities can be ruled out? So, that's it then: the end, the late, great, human race finally gone and there is NOTHING left in the near limitless universe?

That said, it is equally worrying to consider that there almost certainly are other races out there and they might not like us at all. Let's face it, our track record is far from good and we have some truly deplorable tendencies like resorting to violence, mass destruction and cruelty for whatever reason. Perhaps we should not be too anxious to make our presence known to other races in the universe by deliberately sending out radio signals and space craft bearing information about us (assuming that they would be found and the message understood).

This possibility introduces the ultimate question: who sent the 'packets' and why did they send them? But before we look at this there is yet another question. According to our cosmology the universe in which we live came into being at the beginning of time when the 'Big Bang' occurred and the constituent parts of the universe erupted from the miniscule singularity at its core. From what is known – or perhaps hypothesised might be a better description – of this event, it is assumed that the matter forming the universe and all it contains was created in literally nanoseconds from the super-dense core singularity. Does this mean that all the gases, elements and particles arrived in their places uniformly and at the same instant?

We know this is not the case, because many millions of planets and stars are of various ages and the Earth is relatively young in planetary terms (e.g. our sun is still in its robust early middle age); so we can safely assume that there are planets and suns out there that are very much older. This also applies to suns in other galaxies, many of which long ago used up their fuel and burned out and are in the process of collapsing to create 'black holes'. In fact we can sometimes witness the destruction of stars in the form of novas and supernovas, safe in the knowledge that they are trillions and billions of miles away, separated from our solar system in distances measured in light years.

So, who sent the 'packets' and why? Is it possible that they were sent by beings not too unlike us, because they knew that as a species they were ultimately facing extinction? From their point of view perhaps the best option was to give themselves the best possible chance for survival *as a species* and fire these 'life-packets' out in their tens of millions and hope for the best. This hypothetical race had to be like us in most respects simply because the materials they sent out could only turn into DNA in a specific set of circumstances and those circumstances can only be found on our universe, specifically in a star system with very specific parameters...like ours.

The truth is that right now, if we really wanted to, we could do exactly the same thing but could it ever be justified? There have been science fiction stories portraying the human race as a plague, a self-replicating infestation to be eliminated at all costs and based on our history it is not difficult to see why. Curiously it is this point that produces an unlikely alliance of the hard core theists who believe that their God did it all and the rabid rationalists who maintain that sentient life is a process of ongoing evolution and natural selection. Both camps vehemently refute any possibility that directed panspermia is even worthy of discussion, yet the arguments for this view are extremely seductive.

The Anthropic Principle.

Before continuing it might be reasonable to return to something mentioned earlier, and that is 'The Goldilocks Zone', or the fact that Planet Earth seems purposely designed to support life in the form we recognise it. We have already seen that everything is absolutely right to sustain life, right down to the light, heat, gravity, atmosphere, radiation and everything else that goes with it, it is as if the universe (never mind our small solar system) was fine tuned to create life. This once again comes back to the thorny question of; created by what or whom? All of which lead to the idea of the 'Anthropic Principle' and even here there are two variations. One of these is the 'strong anthropic principle' that insists that the universe was forced by some unknown means to cause the appearance of intelligent life.

The 'strong anthropic principle' or 'SAP', states that because of all the interacting intimate forces the Universe has no choice and is compelled in some sense to allow conscious life to eventually emerge. However, critics of the theory promote, not a refutation, but a different version called (unsurprisingly) a 'weak anthropic principle' or 'WAP'. This theory suggests that the apparent 'fine tuning' to permit life is the result of 'selection bias'. This tends to get rather head-spinning and says that only in a universe that can produce intelligent life will beings capable of actually measuring this fine tuning exist. What it all boils down to is this; the universe does not fit us, but rather we fit the universe; not a 'happy accident' exactly, but something close to it.

The really odd thing about this apparent 'fine tuning' is that nowhere else in physics does it appear, why? I have no idea, but it does, which is why the argument still rages in spite of the best efforts of people like Richard Dawkins and of course the latest 'poster boy' of rationalism, Prof Brian Cox, to debunk it. Another way of looking at the subject is this: if the human race has developed sufficiently technically to unravel the mysteries regarding the mechanics of creation to the point where we could produce the first fully functioning human being, would that give us the same knowledge as God? In fact would we even need one? Actually if one takes it the other way round, that answer is we would, because although the human race might succeed in creating the first truly synthetic human being, it would have a very long way to go before it could create another universe.

Talking of which, certain Christian biblical sources give the date of the Creation as 4004 BC, the Creationists have it at 10,000 BC and some Jewish sources are slightly different (and are the most recent), placing it at 3760 BC. All of these dates are drawn from scriptural references and all require that the person(s) interpreting the information believe absolutely in the validity of scripture, despite the abundant evidence proving exactly the opposite. In other words that the bible is 100% correct (it is after all by their standards the revealed word of God) and the scientific evidence in spite of the abundant and proven evidence is wrong on every count. This is another, slightly more modern example of the Scopes Monkey Trials all over again and is avidly promoted by fundamentalist sects; it is called 'faith' and is quite unarguable.

Chapter Six
Hiding in Plain Sight?

We are part of a symbiotic relationship with something which disguises itself as an extra-terrestrial invasion so as not to alarm us." These insightful and profound words taken from a lecture by the late pioneering ethno-botanist, philosopher and fearless psychonaught Dr Terrence McKenna, should perhaps sound a warning to those who have wrapped themselves in the insulating blanket of their own beliefs. This includes a full spectrum of people ranging from died-in-the-wool Ufologists to those with deeply held religious convictions, and the strange thing is that, depending on one's perspective, they are not all that far apart, because both schools of thought depend, in the main, on faith.

Another prominent researcher into similar matters is the astrophysicist, Ufologist, mathematician and (oddly enough) venture capitalist the French born Dr Jacques Vallee whose ideas mirror those of Dr McKenna. According to Dr Vallee when speaking about the subject of UFO's, *'This is an age old and worldwide myth that has shaped our belief structures, our scientific expectations and our view of ourselves. I do not use the word, 'myth', here to mean something that is imaginary, but on the contrary, something that is at such a deep level that it influences the very basic elements of our thoughts'*.

Both of these researchers hint strongly at something so profound and innate that we cannot distance ourselves far enough from it to see it for what it is. That said, especially from the observations of Terrence McKenna, since both men appear to imply that the relationship is probably symbiotic and not parasitic, then if nothing else it is not necessarily harmful and may in fact be ultimately beneficial.

The Fatima Phenomenon.

The troubling thing is why would these entities choose to disguise themselves, is there something so potentially alarming about them that they have to do this, or is the concealment for a much more subtle reason? If, as has been suggested in several quarters, some major spiritual events such as appearances of the Blessed Virgin Mary (BVM) are UFO related manifestations, then does this also mean that, once again drawing inferences from Dr McKenna's quotation, that whatever these 'forces of Heaven' consist of (if that is what they are) they may not be suitable for human eyes?

This seems to blend harmoniously with Dr Vallee's ideas, so perhaps one instance where the UFO connection is almost unavoidable is the 'Miracle of Fatima', therefore we should perhaps look at this and the events surrounding it. The occurrence, which, while it carries the Catholic Churches' seal of approval, could easily be interpreted to infer the involvement of extraterrestrial/inter-dimensional entities. The incident specifically involves Marian Visions (supernatural images of the BVM), plus prophecies and secrets, which could equally apply to contact with beings that are not from this Earth.

In fact, the so-called 'space brothers' of the 1950's also continually warned of humanities imminent demise, so are they in effect one and the same thing? If one thinks about it humanities self-immolation was a common theme in this era and also found expression in the iconic and paranoid 1950's Cold-War Sci-Fi parable, 'The Day the Earth Stood Still', when an altruistic 'space ambassador' arrived to warn of an potential nuclear holocaust caused by the east/west face off. Unfortunately he was shot and critically wounded for his pains and only survived thanks to the combined efforts of a friendly human female, his faithful (and immensely powerful and deadly) robot 'bodyguard' and a remarkable piece of alien medical technology.

The Miracle of Fatima concerned a series of appearances and prophecies made to three children, Jacinta and Francisco Marto and Lucia dos Santos near the village of Fatima in Portugal on May 13th, 1879. The children claimed that, *'A beautiful lady from Heaven'* told them to meet her at the same spot on the 13th of each month until October that year. Naturally this began attracting crowds of the faithful and the curious, some of whom claimed to see a cloud where the children could see the vision. Eventually the local authorities spent two days questioning the children, although bullying might be a better description, but they did not change their story. On the 13th of August, the children received another vision of the 'Beautiful Lady', this time at Valhinos, which is near Fatima. She reminded them that they would see her for the last time on the 13th of October and we should keep in mind using the ET/dimensional paradigm that the 'space brothers' also made prearranged rendezvous.

When October the 13th finally arrived, some 50,000 people assembled around the grotto, however, when 'the lady' materialised once again she was visible only to the children. This time she said she was *'Our Lady of the Rosary'* and she had three secrets concerning the future to tell them. According to dozens of accounts at this point the rain that had been falling steadily suddenly stopped and the sun came out. Accompanied by a humming sound the sun began to spin then plunged towards the earth, this occurred three times then everything returned to normal. Is this a description of bizarre celestial mechanics or something else? If thousands of people witnessed the sun dipping to the horizon and returning to the sky three times in quick succession, then it is likely that they witnessed not the sun, but a spacecraft manoeuvring. Some of those present also noticed that their previously wet clothing had dried out; heat? Yes, perhaps, but caused by what, the sun or something else? Close proximity to microwave or similar radiation perhaps?

The tale of what occurred at Fatima still draws pilgrims by the thousand to view the area where all this happened and predictably it also engenders its fair share of alleged miracles. As far as the information contained in the supposed secrets is concerned, there has never been any really satisfactory explanation of what was in them other than visions of Hell in the first secret, vague generalisations about wars and rumours of wars in the second. However, the third foretold of the oppression of Christianity in the 20th century and the attempted assassination of a pope.

That said; the late author, Jesuit and sometime exorcist, Fr Malachi Martin, was convinced that it foretold of division within the fabric of the Church itself. The warning of division and fragmentation was accompanied by the inference that the final pope would be influenced by Satan; unsurprisingly this was something that the Holy See, and especially the Curia, was keen to suppress. It has further been suggested that the original hand written account of the Third Secret given by Lucia dos Santos comprised only one page, while the 'official version' comprised four. Why the extra padding?

Cardinal Joseph Ratzinger (formerly Pope Benedict the XIV) at that time the head of the Congregation for the Doctrine of the Faith – the former Holy Inquisition – pronounced upon the 'secret' in 1980 implying that it foretold of Armageddon and the End Times. Bear in mind though that all of this should be viewed in the context of the approaching year 2000 and all the fearful predictions of planetary upheavals that (fortunately) never materialised. We should also remember that it may have served the interests of the Church to keep the faithful afraid and therefore compliant. Could this possibly hint that whatever this invisible but ubiquitous 'something' that conceals itself from us acts through faith based power brokers to carry out its inscrutable bidding. Once again the entire affair is shrouded in mystery and no small amount of secrecy and (deliberate?) obfuscation.

Lourdes

Another supposed supernatural appearance and one that is, if anything, better known than the occurrences at Fatima was the appearance of an entity in a near the town of Lourdes. The entity was eventually given the seal of approval by the Catholic Church as the Mother of God, the Blessed Virgin Mary; however a closer look at the facts reveals something rather different. Incidentally, the fact that miracles apparently happened (and evidently sometimes still do) does not of course guarantee that the entity was necessarily 'sacred' or 'holy', because as we shall see the description of what was seen also translates in the local patios as a 'fairy'. The sighting that triggered the furore in Lourdes, and indeed reverberated around the world, took place early in 1858 in what was a relatively insular and extremely traditional area in the Pyrenees. Indeed it demonstrates just how primitive the area was when one considers that a witch burning had occurred in a nearby town only five years earlier in 1851.

The grotto in which the sighting occurred is also known as the 'Cave of Massabielle' and forms part of a series of grottos, some of which reach deep into the mountainside creating large caverns. More importantly the area already had a long standing and rich tradition relating to supernatural occurrences and sightings and it was also a location that even then held deep, although tacit, sympathy for the Cathars and their belief system of Gnostic

Christianity. In relation to the phenomena that took place in the grotto, the local people also held traditional belief in the reality of wizards and demons and in particular the '*fees*' (or fairies) that were always called 'white ladies'.

Typically, these entities appear to share similar character traits with beings sometimes known as '*the faerie*' and are at best indifferent to human beings and at worst wholly inimical. In fact the area around the Cave of Massabielle was in many ways notorious for its magickal associations and as a result it was in any case treated with great respect by the superstitious locals who tended to shun it, especially after nightfall. However, after the sighting on the 11th of February 1858 that perception changed markedly.

The initial sighting was made by young Bernadette Soubirous when she, her sister Toinette and a female friend became separated while walking close to the grottos. The accepted version of events tells that Bernadette fell behind the other two and after watching them cross a narrow stream she was unsure whether to follow them or not. As she deliberated she heard a 'whooshing' noise, like the sound of a rush of wind, then looking around her she spotted a figure dressed in white standing in a niche in the grotto; the vision evidently entranced her. When Bernadette's friends realised that she was missing they returned and saw her kneeling, totally unaware of them.

Suddenly she roused from her trance and although her friends were concerned for her they all returned home. However, on hearing what had occurred at the grotto the response from Bernadette's parents was one of annoyance and her mother beat her saying she must be mistaken. Her mother was convinced that the figure was the soul of one of their relatives in purgatory and had to be prayed for. The idea of purgatory as a place for purification and the expiation of sins is a concept that predates Christianity, but was adopted and formalised by the Catholic Church in series of church councils ending with the 16th century Council of Trent.

In spite of her parent's reactions, Bernadette returned to the grotto where she continued to see the 'white lady' although the friends who went with her could still see nothing. It is important to realise that at that time there was still no official connection made with the BVM and the locals were concerned that this entity might be a ghost. They had even decided that the entity was actually the recently deceased leader of a prayer group, the Children of Mary. She was also held in high regard by the locals who regarded her as something of a saint. The mode of dress adopted by the prayer group was a white robe with a blue girdle, exactly the same colouring used to depict what was eventually mooted as the Virgin Mary.

The entity was asked (via Bernadette) if it was in fact the dead woman, but evidently no answer was forthcoming. The consensus was that while not necessarily evil neither was the entity the Virgin Mary (*or 'The Dame' as she became known*). However, as time passed and the Church deliberated, the tales took on a life of their own and by popular consent the entity eventually morphed into the BVM with not a shred of evidence to back this up. Incidentally, the Children of Mary does exist within the Catholic Church, but as an adjunct to an order of nuns, the Sisters of Charity, and predates the Lourdes sightings.

In short order other people, mainly children, began to experience trance states and visions at the grotto, perhaps they did, but in these cases the 'beautiful lady' was not static and appeared floating above the ground. This vision evidently had less than pure motives and tried to entice those who saw it to follow it over the edge of cliffs or into fast running waters. In addition, glowing orbs were also observed floating in and around the grotto as if enticing those who saw them to follow. More worryingly the people who had these particular visions gave every indication that they were possessed. Anyway, whatever the truth of the matter the entire series of events became mired in a cloak of propaganda, which for obvious reasons, the Catholic Church encouraged. The next obvious question is, if not religious totems what were the entities seen at Lourdes and of course Fatima?

Some of the evidence, the 'whooshing noise' prior to the first sighting at Lourdes for example suggests a rapid displacement of air; perhaps something materialised or maybe a sudden vacuum was created. This effect has also been noted by some individuals who assert that they have been on board extraterrestrial spacecraft. The initial reaction in both Fatima and Lourdes was that what had been seen was not in any way sacred, but rather quite the opposite. The actions attributed to the sun at Fatima are physically impossible, (although to ultra-faithful zealots this is not a problem because their version of God can do anything). The fact that the 'entities' could only been seen by a very limited number of people is not unknown in UFO encounters either, the similarities go on. The one thing that is unknowable is why? Why the concealment and why the 'behind the scenes' machinations?

We opened with a quotation and it is fitting that we end with one; Charles Fort once commented that, *'The Earth is a farm. We are someone else's property'*. This astute observation was made by a man who devoted his life to collecting and tabulating the bizarre, the anomalous and the strange and even he was eventually drawn to the conclusion that occasionally things that happen are so utterly strange and unlikely that they cannot be attributed to sheer coincidence or happenstance. Many of those happenings are now gathered under the convenient heading of 'synchronicity', a term invented by Carl Gustav Yung to cover coincidences and other events that occur, which by all logic should have absolutely no connection, but nevertheless still occur.

Chapter Seven
The Extraterrestrial Hypothesis and the Periodic Table

The Extraterrestrial Hypothesis (ETH) is one of the sacred cows of Ufology and like all fervently held beliefs it carries with it certain articles of faith, these articles of faith are based around certain events deemed to prove beyond all doubt that we as a species have been visited by non-human extraterrestrial entities (ET's for short) since the beginning of time. This opinion is of course perfectly correct…and at the same time utterly wrong for valid reasons that we will consider shortly. First we should examine some very powerful examples that seem to prove the existence of encounters with extraterrestrials.

I could fill page after page with these accounts, so I will quote only those comparatively recent events that have resonated strongly with believers. I should add that the list is entirely arbitrary and in no particular order regarding dates and it does not include reports of actual contact with the occupants of the craft, it may provoke some controversy, but hopefully the cases are representative of the genre. While I do not offer any rationalist alternative explanation for all the sightings mentioned here, in addition to quoting the bare bones of what was reported at the time and has since become part of ETH dogma, in the second example in particular I offer what appears to be an entirely credible alternative explanation.

The many reports of so-called 'Foo Fighters', small, agile balls of light that appeared during the Second World War and closely followed the movements of both bombers and fighter aircraft. They were assumed to be some kind of German secret weapon, but their origin is still officially unknown.

The famous 1947 Kenneth Arnold sighting of unusual craft as he piloted his small aircraft close to Mount Rainier in Washington State. Arnold claims to have seen objects that skipped like 'pie plates' or 'pie dishes' and even 'like fishes flipping in the sun'. We will take a look at this event in some detail because it is one of the true icons that defined modern Ufology as we know it and was this very incident that both gave rise to the long lasting epithet 'flying saucer' and also helped prod the US government into instituting Project Sign to investigate the incident. This of course developed into Project Grudge and ultimately culminated in the 1952

Project Blue Book, which was an attempt by the USAF to look at the phenomenon in as detached a manner as possible. Project Grudge had been created with a distinctly debunking agenda; the name said it all really. Blue Book had the astronomer, Dr Allen Hynek, as its scientific advisor. It was Hynek who came up with the famous categories of 'close encounter' categorised, depending to the degree of closeness and contact with the assumed ET, as being of the 1st, 2nd, 3rd and 4th kind.

However, what Kenneth Arnold actually saw was probably not extraterrestrial at all, highly exotic yes, classified yes, but given what he claims to have seen (he is shown in several pictures standing beside one of the illustrations), it was more likely to have been an experimental aircraft based on flying wing designs developed by the Horten brothers in Germany before and during WWII. The Hortens were both members of the Hitler Youth movement and both also became pilots in the Luftwaffe as well, although most of their time was devoted to developing and improving their unique designs.

As mentioned earlier these blueprints and in fact a complete airframe were taken under the auspices of Project Paperclip and given to the Northrop Aircraft Company who already had some experience with flying wing designs. The picture most associated with what Arnold saw is a scalloped, flying wing design and some very basic research reveals that it is almost identical in appearance to the Horten Ho229 jet fighter, sometimes dubbed 'Hitler's stealth fighter'.

This is especially true if one looks at what Northrop produced when they actually built one of the Horten craft. As previously mentioned, other designs from the Hortens were also taken to the USA and one of them, the HoVIII the so-called 'Amerika Bomber', appeared later as the Northrop YB49 flying wing bomber for the US air force. Although not especially successful in this form Northrop persisted and finally produced the B2 Spirit bomber which is still very much in service.

It is sometime pointed out that Arnold reported that what he saw was flying at 10,000 ft at an estimated speed of 1,200 mph, and this speed was assumed to be beyond any known design around at that time. This is quite right, it was, but the emphasis is on the word 'known'. However it is recognised that many of the military aircraft flying today began as highly secret projects, in some cases inaugurated twenty years before they were revealed to the public.

If that is the case, what Arnold saw were not ET spacecraft, but were almost certainly highly secret experimental aircraft that may, or indeed may not, have emerged into the public gaze many years later, for in some cases experimental aircraft never actually make it into final production. An example of this was the CIA funded 1962 race to develop the aircraft that eventually became the SR71 Blackbird made by Lockheed at their super-secret 'skunk works'.

The American firm, Convair, was tendering for the same contract and produced another remarkable design called 'Kingfish', a truly remarkable looking triangular aircraft that had a roughly similar performance. However Lockheed was the winner and produced one of the most purposeful, strangely beautiful yet menacing flying machines ever manufactured. It has to be said that, based on what it looks like, the Convair design might even have ended up as the legendary 'Aurora'; another officially denied and long standing 'black project'. We should keep in mind that just because one particular design does not meet requirements at that time it would still comprise highly classified elements and might well re-appear in a slightly different form elsewhere. This is before we consider older designs like the U2 which, due to its shiny finish, was a source of many UFO sightings in the 1950's. These sightings dropped off markedly when the craft was painted matt grey and amazingly, after nearly 60 years the U2 is still in service unlike the SR71, which was finally retired in 1998.

The Captain Thomas Mantell incident from 1948 where three P51 fighter aircraft were scrambled from Godman AFB to investigate a suspected UFO, perhaps significantly none of the aircraft had oxygen on board. Two of the P51's broke off the pursuit due to the altitude and the speed of the object, but unfortunately Capt. Mantell did not and his aircraft was seen to dive towards the ground, disintegrate a few thousand feet above ground then crash, Capt. Mantell was later found dead among the wreckage.

The Farmington UFO sightings where, in 1950, the skies over Los Alamos national Laboratories (LANL) in New Mexico were filled with strange aircraft ranging in number from 'a few' to 'hundreds'. LANL is where much of the original US atomic energy programme was developed and it is not far for other key areas like Dulce, where stories and allegations about underground bases concealing aliens are legion.

The incident from 1978 on the 39th and 31st of December when an Australian TV crew, who were aboard a New Zealand based freight aircraft attempting to film UFO's that were appearing in the area at the time, actually filmed something rapidly approaching the aircraft. The sightings occurred over two nights and were confirmed on ground radar.

Then of course there are the occurrences at Gulf Breeze, the Phoenix Lights, Rendlesham Forest in England (still the scene of many alleged encounters with entities of various kinds) and even the village of Bonnybridge in central Scotland. Then of course there is the granddaddy of them all, Roswell New Mexico and all the fanfare that still surrounds it, and indeed the lucrative careers that have been built on this single event, although Rendlesham runs it a very close second in terms of fame and/or notoriety.

And so it goes: all examples of the cognitive dissonance mentioned at the start of this book, incident after incident and in spite of the convincing evidence to the contrary as in the Kenneth Arnold sighting, all supplying its own distinctive and unarguable morsel of 'proof' to the believers. The selection of accounts quoted here are only those that do not involve actual (and surprisingly frequent) alleged contact with the occupants of the craft. These incidents are only a few of the apparently non-negotiable articles of faith upon which the ETH is based, and, like it or not, they are all seriously flawed. Before anyone denounces me as a vile and sacrilegious heretic to the self-appointed UFO Inquisition I should make one thing abundantly clear. I have no absolutely no quibble whatsoever, none, with the idea that we are visited by non-human and probably non-terrestrial entities, but I have serious and possibly valid doubts concerning the dogma lying at the heart of the ETH.

How do the ET's Get Here?

There are a number of reasons for this, the most obvious one being this: supposed ET spaceship hidden in bases on the Moon aside, since these entities are presumably arriving from some point outside our solar system this must, indeed has to, involve interstellar travel. According to our present understanding of physics this must necessitate velocities greater than the speed of light and according to the old standard, Einstein's E=MC2, (which if anyone is interested means E=energy, equals M=mass and C= the speed of light), so the energy required equals mass times the speed of light squared.

Therefore, as one approaches the speed of light mass becomes infinite and correspondingly requires infinite energy to drive it. According to the equation this is impossible to achieve so there has to be another solution, actually modern science has partly disproved what Einstein said, but the practical results of this are still some way down the line. Besides, and again by our understanding of how this might work, such speeds involve time travel and this at least has been partially proven using our own comparatively clunky technology. So, logically, if ET uses superluminal speeds then according to our physics ET is also a time traveller.

The alternative to this is to actually fold space and in effect 'travel without moving', something that was used to good effect in the Frank Herbert classic Sci-Fi novel and film 'Dune' where the Guild Navigators folded space to permit instant transit from one part on the galaxy to another (oh, if only). Our current understanding of physics, and I stress 'current', actually allows for this and indeed it is at least feasible, however the level of technology we have at present makes it untenable. To do so would involve creating an intense, rotating gravity field to warp space/time which would pull the destination to the front of the vessel and allow it to pass through and in effect travel interstellar distances without have physically moved at all. Voodoo science to be sure but still theoretically possible.

One Possible Solution

Some of the more outré means by which ET supposedly gets here is via a worm-hole cum Stargate device that warps space time and opens a 'tunnel' direct to where you want to go. It has been speculated that for no good or obvious reason the aforementioned village of Bonnybridge in central Scotland is on the receiving end of one of these artefacts. However, according to the accompanying lore, these stargate/portals are not fixed and can be redirected at the whim of whoever operates them, which is why the UFO flap at Bonnybridge faded and died. All of this is well and good, but it all relies on different varieties of 'voodoo technology' that we cannot yet define and currently can only guess at and apparently for reasons of expediency little if any credence is given to the possibility that ET simply does not exist at all *in this universe*.

So, if not in this universe then where? Let's look at one basic ingredient of science that has been around since at least 1869, i.e. the periodic table. The periodic table consists of 118 elements beginning with the most common, Hydrogen. These elements (discovered so far) are what constitutes the planet Earth and everything and everyone on it. If one subscribes to the 'Big Bang' theory as the beginning of the cosmos, then it follows that these elements must have originated right there and then and what's more they must be present more or less uniformly throughout the universe, they have to be. So, if as we are frequently told, that our visitors sometimes leave behind traces of their presence in the form of artefacts of utterly unknown origin consisting of unknown elements then where did they come from?

If they came from this universe with its 118 known elements (although this is subject to change on a regular basis, there have been claims that there are as many as 122 elements) then surely we would recognise them, if they did not then is it not reasonable to suggest that they did not come from this universe at all? It follows then that if these elements did not originate in this universe then neither did the entities that brought them, this would at least satisfy the glaring gaps in the logic of the ETH and it would answer most, if not all, of the problems created by their means of transport. One possible addition to this hypothesis is that at least some ET's and their vehicles have many of the characteristics of ghosts and other examples of supernatural beings, that being the case might 'ghosts' (or their equivalents, the '*shadow people*') also inhabit this invisible, but still accessible, realm?

The one downside to this hypothesis, while it does provide one logical point of origin for ET's and all the rest is this; it does not provide an answer regarding how 'they' actually traverse the interface between their version of reality and ours. This is yet another perplexing conundrum we have yet to solve (if indeed we ever do), but at least we now have a feasible explanation that sits well with all shades of believer. Yes, we are visited by non-terrestrial beings, but they almost certainly do not originate in this version of the universe and now, perhaps, we can see why.

One last word about the periodic table, the last of the 118 elements was only identified in 2003 and synthesised in 2006, but theoretically there can be more than this. However although it has been hypothesised that there could be as many as 173 elements, only 1 to 94 of the 118 exists naturally on Earth and as for the hypothetical elements reaching to 173, some of these would require that their components would have to exist at more than the speed of light, which according to most current thinking makes their existence an impossibility.

PART TWO
Everyday Magick

Chapter Eight
Christ, The Shroud and The Rainbow Body

T his chapter is an attempt to cast fresh light and understanding on one of the most mysterious and enigmatic spiritual artefacts still in existence, the image on the Shroud of Turin. In order to do this we have to consider the apparently disparate roles of science and spirituality, because the truths inherent in one may cast some useful implications on the other. Once we start looking at the Shroud without the baggage of religious dogma or preconceptions, it becomes evident that this faint image and how it was produced may, surprisingly, not necessarily be without precedent. We also have to assume that it is genuine, because my research indicates that there is a strong possibility that it may be, but, vitally, not for the reasons normally given. This might also reveal a little more about the nature and background of Jesus Christ, his abilities, and what he actually was.

One of the most powerful and evocative Christian religious artefacts ever revealed to the public gaze is, almost certainly, the Shroud of Turin; the length of plain linen fabric that supposedly enveloped the brutalised and crucified body of Jesus Christ, upon whose teachings and philosophy the Christian religion is founded. What makes this funeral wrapping so special is that it bears an uncanny, utterly lifelike photographic negative image (both front and back) of a man who has clearly suffered a great deal of physical trauma in the time before he died. The image is claimed (in the main by the Roman Catholic Church), to be the body of Jesus Christ. This winding sheet was allegedly used to wrap His body when, after His eventual death on the hill of Calvary, he was washed and laid out in the nearby unoccupied tomb of His uncle, Joseph of Arimathea.

The fourteen-foot long piece of new linen cloth used was all that remained after his body was found to have mysteriously vanished from the tomb. The morning after his burial, his mother Mary accompanied by Mary Magdalene, visited the tomb and found the rock covering the entrance had already been rolled back and a stranger, who was present in the tomb, told the two women that Christ had returned to God his father. The women claimed that the stranger was an angel. Whether or not this is true is almost secondary to the existence of the Shroud, it is however a rather neat way to tidy up any loose ends and is one sure way to explain the disappearance of the body. It also created a precedent for notions such as 'The Rapture', when true believers, mostly evangelical Christians, will be literally whisked off their feet and lifted bodily into Heaven.

Among the many suggestions made is that, the dualist Gnostic beliefs aside, Christ did not die on the cross and made his escape with the assistance of friends and the burial was a ruse, or, he did die and the body was simply removed elsewhere for safekeeping. The reason for its removal would have been entirely pragmatic from the Roman perspective, because as long as the body was accessible then it might be used to foment further unrest. It was for similar reasons that the bodies of the Nazi demagogue Adolph Hitler and also the idolised Argentinean, Eva Peron, were never allowed to fall into the hands of sympathisers.

It has, however, been argued that the story of Jesus' burial is entirely fictitious, because, as a rule, the Romans denied anyone who had been crucified the dignity of a decent and dignified burial. Since crucifixion was, after all, their most heinous form of execution reserved for the worst offenders, they considered that anyone whose behaviour had, in their view, merited such a punishment did not deserve any respect at all. As a result of this, bodies removed from the cross were normally thrown into a mass grave or pit. If Jesus did escape this fate then it indicates that either his supporters wielded considerable influence, or he was not dead.

The winding sheet itself first appeared in the public domain when, in 1347, it was displayed in a church in the town of Liray in France. The Shroud had previously been in the charge of the de-Charney family, although there is no explanation of how it came into their possession. Due to the nature of this relic it might be more appropriate to refer to those who possess this artefact as its guardians or keepers rather than its owners; a view that may become relevant as we consider some of the alternative possibilities. A few months after its initial exposition, perhaps significantly, the bishop of Troyes declared it to be a painting and therefore a fake and ordered its destruction. However, for some reason the Shroud was not destroyed and stayed hidden with the de-Charneys until circa 1453 when it came under the protection of the Savoy family. The winding sheet was sold, or perhaps bartered would be a better term, to Duke Louis of Savoy, who was the son of Pope Felix V, for two castles.

The Savoy's, who still actually retain the legal stewardship of the Shroud, after some consultations and negotiations decided to have it kept in the Cathedral of St John the Baptist in Turin where it lies in the Chapel of the Holy Shroud. As most people will be well aware, this piece of fabric bears a unique image of the body that it allegedly covered, the image is generally assumed to be that of Jesus Christ. It should be made clear that religions, all religions, like nothing better than relics of their key figures for the purely pragmatic reason that it strengthens belief, and there is no more important a figurehead for Christianity than a relic of Jesus Christ.

Due to the nature of this artefact, proof of its authenticity is vital and there have been no shortage of individuals and organisations eager to, by turns, either prove or disprove its validity. There have been many competing theories and techniques employed in this process, each one making claim and counterclaim regarding the authenticity of the cloth and in particular the identity of the image. The tests included everything from microscopic inspection of the cloth and carbon dating, to possible DNA profiling of the blood flows left on the cloth from the crucifixion wounds.

Some claim that it is indeed that of the crucified Christ, somehow miraculously imprinted on the virgin material, others aver that it is in fact nothing else but a photographic image of Leonardo daVinci. They cite the fact that there is a clear demarcation between the head and the body of the Shroud image, i.e. it is not attached, then demonstrating that the face is nearly identical to that of certain portraits of Leonardo. I have actually been privileged to witness this technique demonstrated at a presentation given by the noted authors and researchers Clive Prince and Lynn Picknett using computers and 'morphing' technology and the similarities between Leonardo's face and the Shroud image are indeed startling. It should be added that Prince and Picknett strongly advocate the hypothesis that the image on the shroud is a photographic image and have conducted experiments using materials that would have been available to daVinci showing that their idea is a practical proposition. We should also keep in mind that daVinci was an extremely able and highly intelligent man, so the idea cannot be entirely discounted.

Although the carbon14 dating technique employed in 1989 established that the Shroud dates from around 1260 to 1380, evidence from the pro-Shroud camp has since emerged stating that these tests were flawed and conducted on sections of the Shroud that had been repaired in 1534 using material from that era. Although feasible, it seems unlikely that those who took the samples should have done this, since they must have been well aware that the repaired sections were of a different date. The only way that this could have happened was if those supervising the removal of the samples had an agenda and wanted it to happen. It is certain that those who are convinced of the Shroud's authenticity would have ensured that the main body of the material was sampled.

The image itself has to be contentious, because no one knows with any degree of certainty what Christ actually looked like, although there is another artefact supposedly bearing His likeness and that is The Veil of Veronica. The Veil of Veronica, or Sudarium, sometimes referred to simply as 'The Veronica', is a fabric relic supposedly bearing an image of Christ's face produced when St Veronica wiped away the sweat and blood from His face as He struggled and staggered under the weight of the cross along the way to Calvary.

It has to be said that this artefact long precedes the Shroud and is, unlike the Shroud, supposedly able to produce miraculous cures, but more significantly the image it bears looks nothing like the face on the Shroud. In fact recent forensic tests using cutting-edge techniques, which compare points on the eye sockets, nose and lips, indicated that the faces are not representations of the same person. What is however of supreme importance is how the image on the Shroud was actually produced, and if, as has been suggested in some quarters, the image was produced by a burst of 'radiation' of some kind, then we are bordering on the edge of a strange kind of technology, (for want of a better word).

Where it becomes problematic is whether this technology was science based or truly 'miraculous' i.e. produced by some entirely unknown process akin to magick, because in some cases there is absolutely no difference except, as always, in the context. If the image actually was formed by a mysterious surge or burst of radiation, then what was it and where did it come from? Did it appear due to some miraculous/magickal act orchestrated and initiated by God? Because if it did, then if we could determine the source of the radiation and the type, then we may even be able to catch a glimpse into Gods laboratory. This seems to parallel an observation made by the physicist Stephen Hawking when he said: *"If we do discover a theory of everything...it would be the ultimate triumph of human reason—for then we would truly know the mind of God."*

If on the other hand the radiation was not from God, but from a much more earthly, but still remarkable source, then who might have been behind it? The enigmatic Knights Templar certainly had the money, resources, knowledge, motivation and ambition to carry out such a project, but would they have had the patience? We have already seen how modern forensic techniques were used to compare two images ostensibly showing the face of Jesus, but the technology does not stop there. Using computer scanning and imaging techniques a complete three-dimensional image has been created showing a life-like reproduction of the Shroud image. So far this is confined to the memory banks of a computer, but using the same techniques and a big enough 3D printer it would not be difficult to create a full sized life model of the body.

The real, in fact the *only* key to the puzzle, is of course the original source of the image, in other words what created it? If it is not, as has been eloquently suggested in some quarters, a primitive but extremely long lasting and effective photographic image; if it is not a painting, if it was not caused by the fluids from the corpse reacting with the cloth, then what is it? If it was, as has been implied by the Catholic Church, an image produced by the process of Christ's resurrection, then what was it and how could that have been achieved and is there any parallel for such an event? Surprisingly the answer is yes, there are two, the first is the truly bizarre phenomenon known as 'The Rainbow Body'.

The Rainbow Body

The so-called 'rainbow body' is a final state of nirvanic perfection allegedly achieved when the human body of someone, normally a Buddhist adept, who has mastered the techniques necessary to achieve absolute spiritual perfection dies. This is not easy to explain let alone understand, but what occurs involves the practitioners of the *Dzogchen* strain of Tibetan Buddhism. The elements that compose their bodies, at the point of physical death, return to a primordial spiritual essence involving five pure lights of the elemental processes. It also involves a sort of conscious and deliberate 'mindstream' created by another meditation technique called *'phowa'*, this is a truly remarkable procedure involving the deliberate transference of consciousness and self at the time of death.

If this sounds complicated and obscure that is because it is and only a very, very few individuals have actually mastered the technique. Among the adepts who have allegedly managed to achieve this remarkable state are Shug-gseb Je-btsun Cho-nyid bzang-mo, Kenchen Tsewang Rigdzin, (who was last seen in 1958), Khenpo A-chos and Shardza Tashi Gyaltsen. The last of this quartet of initiates was also an exponent of the 'Bonpo' tradition of Buddhism, which incorporates eclectic, animistic and shamanic elements into an already heady mix of traditions.

The effect of this transference is the appearance of coloured lights like a flickering rainbow over the corpse at the point of death. After death the lights slowly dim and vanish and all that is left are the hair, fingernails and teeth, but the body has completely vanished. It is reported that in some cases the fabric of the robes worn by the dying person bore marks and impressions of the body parts of the wearer. A similar idea, but without the light display, is found other cultures where, for example, an old shaman, either male or female using a form of telepathy is able to 'programme' their young successor with their accumulated experience and knowledge at the moment of their death. This process must be akin to downloading the memory banks of a computer then loading them into a new machine, the similarities are striking and recall that the human brain is essentially (albeit of exquisite complexity) an electrical computing device with outputs that can be measured.

Strangely enough the phenomenon of luminosity is also noted as a sign of (or perhaps a result of) extraordinary piety among especially focussed and single minded members of Christian religious communities in monasteries and convents. However, these displays mainly seem to have occurred to saints during the Dark and Middle Ages when belief in deities was much more literal and relevant than now. Those who are said to have exhibited this mystical illumination are St Philip Neri, St Catherine de Ricci, St Alphonsus Liguori and others including St Ignatius Loyola who founded the Jesuit movement. All of them were seen at various times to actually radiate light to the point where their cells in the monasteries in which they lived were illuminated with no need of candles or other form of illumination; some were actually seen to levitate at the same time. There is a secular example from 1935 concerning an Italian woman called Anna Monaro (known as the luminous woman of Pirano) who, after contracting asthma in 1934, began emitting a blue glow from her chest while asleep.

The phenomenon, which lasted for several weeks, was well attested and even filmed, but no real answer was ever found, but the most popular theory was that the glow was caused by sulphites which are luminescent when exposed to ultraviolet (UV) light. While that is true, there was no known UV source present in her home when she produced the spontaneous luminescence, but she was however extremely religious and observed religious feasts, which may or may not be connected. Other examples of this form of natural bio-luminescence have been noted in some cancers where light is emitted, in one case so much so that it was possible to see the hands on a watch held a meter away. We will return to another aspect of this odd property in some forms of cancer in the next section.

As we have seen in the case of Dzogchen Buddhists, this only involves an extremely tiny percentage of practitioners and it means that the devotee is able to restore their physical body to the universe that supplied the constituent parts in the first place. It is yet another illustration of the ubiquitous and cyclic nature of the universe and how we are indeed at one and as one with it, it is almost as if we are only loaned the building blocks, but have to return them when we have no further use for them. It also shows how eastern belief systems like Buddhism and Hinduism recognise the unique relationship between the human race and the universe in a fashion still largely sidelined by all of the major monotheistic religions. It is extremely difficult for the vast majority of us to understand and nigh on impossible to emulate this process and unfortunately this is still the case and shows no signs of changing any time soon.

What we have seen here may even resonate with the Gnostic and dualistic belief that Christ was another manifestation of the ancient tradition of the dying and rising sun god, which of course eternally rose and set and by so-doing gave life. It would help to further reinforce the idea that Christ consciously gave back his 'energy/essence' to the universe in order that the cycle continued, something that has sense of rightness about it. Before dismissing this as utter nonsense, it is no more a nonsense than accepting the resurrection of Christ and the miracles attributed to Him in the first place; if it is acceptable in one belief system then why not similar manifestations in other beliefs and faiths? There is even some more precedence for these claims in relation to some of the effects of light on human DNA.

Luminous DNA?

The concept of the make up of the human body and light, although at first seeming unlikely, resonates with another perhaps more scientific but little known concept and that is that human DNA seems able to actually store photons, in other words light. The ability of human DNA to store light at specific wavelengths is not a fallacy, but a proven fact and was ably demonstrated as far back as the 1970's by Professor Fritz-Albert Popp, a theoretical biophysicist at the University of Marburg in Germany. Prof. Popp did not set out to look for this phenomenon, but stumbled across the unusual property while researching the effects of exposing carcinogenic cells (i.e. cells that carry or transmit cancer) to ultraviolet (UV) light. He found that carcinogens absorbed the light then reradiated it at a different frequency; non-carcinogenic cells allowed the UV light to pass through unaltered.

This led him to study the phenomenon in depth and he found related research showing that if a living cell was virtually destroyed (99%) by using strong UV light, the same cell could be repaired by the same frequency of UV light, but at a greatly reduced intensity. The process is called 'photo repair' and has been known about (if still not fully understood) for many years. Popp was astonished to discover that the photo-repair process was most effective at a wavelength (or frequency) of 380 nanometres, which was the same frequency that the carcinogens reacted to. From there Popp deduced that cancer cells and photo-repair were linked and for that to happen then the human body had to be producing UV light on its own.

After fighting his corner for some years a device was finally constructed that allowed this near miraculous process to be proven and to his delight it was shown that human (and plant) DNA does indeed produce extremely low levels of light in the form of photons. Further experiments with chemicals that cause the DNA helix to unwind showed that the more it unwound the greater the intensity if light was produced, so there is a clear (and apparently beneficial) link with light and how DNA reacts to it This work was further demonstrated and expanded upon some years later by Dr Peter Gariaev when he isolated a sample of DNA in a small container and exposed it to mild laser light. Using similar measuring equipment to that used by Fritz-Albert Popp, he found that the DNA soaked up the light (as photons) and stored it within its structure. The DNA seemed to be using the light as kind of 'food'; it was actually reacting with and using the light for its own purposes. If DNA was reacting like that to light from an external source, what was occurring within the human body, (or any other body for that matter)?

It does however clearly imply that light is absolutely vital to the function of almost every process one can think of, it even lends credibility to the peculiar and possibly dangerous teachings of 'Jasmuheen' (an Australian woman called Ellen Greve) who formed the 'Breatharian' movement, a cult claiming the ability to live on light alone. Unfortunately a few of her followers have been hospitalised (some have actually died) while trying to do this and the lady herself singularly failed to 'live on light' when tested by an Australian TV company. This involve observing her continually while isolated in a hotel room, but after forty-eight hours she displayed signs of dehydration, stress and high blood pressure and for safety reasons the doctor overseeing the demonstration called a halt before the woman's condition got any worse. Perhaps predictably she claimed the failure was due to 'polluted air' rather than a lack of food or water, as far as is known the test was not repeated

Demonstrations of abilities like these seldom if ever stand up to independent and/or close scrutiny, this is why organisations specialising in debunking claims of the paranormal have considerable success, which does not negate them entirely since there could well be another reason that they tend to fail. Perhaps this has similarities with claims for the so-called 'observer effect', where the inclinations of individuals conducting any given experiment (particularly at the quantum level), can have an effect either positive or negative on that experiment, so perhaps the indifference or scepticism of the film crew produced the negative result. This is not an attempt to justify or explain what occurred, but merely a comment on what can happen. Whatever, the experiment was not repeated and debunking organisations can and do change the goalposts if they think that something they are trying to disprove might actually be valid, and that would never do.

That oddity aside, just what these scientific discoveries relating to how the body uses light and what it means is debatable, but it does at least give some sort of credibility to the idea that through supreme control of the body and its functions this stored light or energy can be deliberately and consciously released. It also seems that if the feats attributed to a few Christian saints and Buddhists actually occurred as described, then the release of the stored energy may well have effects other than a display of lights coloured or otherwise. If, as has also been shown, this discharge of light depending on its intensity and frequency also leaves marks on a suitable material if it is close enough, (like a cloak or shroud), then this might well be what occurred when Christ vanished from the tomb.

He was certainly single-minded enough regarding his purpose, function, spirituality and beliefs and it should be no heresy to suggest that he could well have emulated or pre-empted the meditative techniques employed by Buddhist adepts. If Christ is the template upon which many of the ideals of spirituality are based then it should be no surprise that he was capable of deep and intense meditation. If the literal bodily illumination attributed to lesser beings like monks and nuns can be induced by intense religious meditation and ecstasy, there is no reason to suppose that it was not also produced by Christ.

Perhaps after the Hellish brutality of the crucifixion he decided that enough was enough and deliberately set out to return his essence to the void by consciously inducing this outpouring of energy from his DNA. If so then how could he control the agony and trauma he experienced long enough to concentrate? This too is possible if he was indeed as sufficiently spiritually adept as he seems to have been, because yogis and of course some enlightened Buddhists, can control pain and many other physical and bodily processes too. If this true it gives cause to wonder just what role any Creator God would have in all this.

It might even suggest that, as has often been proposed elsewhere, God is not a separate entity at all, but constitutes the universe from which all life springs and it would make the scriptural claim that Christ 'returned to the father' considerably more literal and understandable. We all do this eventually albeit in a less obvious manner whether through decomposition or cremation, the universe wastes nothing. This line of reasoning makes the hypothesis that the image is in fact a photographic image even more viable, so does this mean that the image, although photographic in appearance, was created not through the use of a primitive chemical photographic process, but as a direct reaction of this 'radiation' with the fabric itself, (perhaps a kind of 'scorch image')?

A more recent attempt to explain the image also came to the conclusion that it was a form of print, but not a photograph as suggested by Picknett and Prince elsewhere in this chapter, and produced because of an unusual chemical reaction between a natural soap-like product made from plants used to wash the original cloth before it was used to cover the corpse, and fluids exuding from the corpse itself. This tends to agree with another similar theory put forward by Lomas and Knight in their excellent book 'The Second Messiah', that the image was produce by stress related chemicals released by the corpse after death combining with the linen, both of the methods were tried and actually produced an image but not as perfect as that on the Shroud. It is as well to make clear that in the case of Lomas and Knight they claim that the image on the Shroud is not in fact that of Christ, but instead is Jacques de Molay the last Grand Master of the Knights Templar; again these are all only hypotheses, albeit very plausible.

The enigma of the Shroud of Turin may never be solved, simply because there is much to lose and there are too many vested interests tied to it, but perhaps we are now a little closer to understanding how the image might have got there. However, there is one final possibility here and it is this: we have already mentioned that there is an element of shamanism involved in this equation and it has been claimed that many of the miracles and abilities attributed to Christ have also been noted in shamans. Indeed it has also been postulated that Jesus was Himself a shaman and tradition tells us that when shamans die they 'return to the sky'.

As we have also seen it is also possible to argue that the more exotic manifestations of Buddhism are near identical to the abilities of shamans. If this is the case we have yet another curious parallel between all mystical and spiritual traditions and the ethereal source hidden at the very fundament of human existence. Are we all creatures of light, are we, as gurus of the New Age tell us 'children of the universe' with all that entails? As always the answers are far from clear, but given the natural curiosity and ingenuity of our species perhaps one day we will find out and a new and vibrant chapter in the saga of the human race will begin.

The 'Deathflash'

As we have seen there are several possibilities regarding how the image may have become imprinted on the shroud, and this is yet another example of the curious relationship between human DNA and light. It shows the spontaneous emission of light following physical death, it is called, perhaps rather dramatically, the 'deathflash'. The hypothesis is taken from Janis Slawinski writing in a 1987 edition of 'The Journal of Near-Death Studies'. In the article, which draws on other work on the natural emission of light by living organisms, Slawinski says that at the point of death, depending on how fast the organism (or person) dies, the 'molecular light' can increase up to one thousand fold in intensity.

He does not make the connection with creating an image from the burst of radiation though, but, instead, assumes that the increase in light noted by those who have had near death experiences may have been caused by this 'deathflash'. He also asserts that this light may hold an immense amount of information. It is interesting to note that the possibility of an intense burst of radiation, in this case light, being released upon death is spontaneous and apparently not solely confined to spiritual adepts.

Chapter Nine
Rock 'n' Magick: Rock Music, the Occult and Advertising

Human beings like to think that they have free will over what they think and do and believe their actions are all due to their own decision making processes. However, this may not always be the case and over the years various techniques have been used to subvert this, some more successfully than others. Not all of these have emanated from shadowy government laboratories, but from other less obvious and totally unexpected quarters. The human race has, since the beginning of time, enjoyed a strange relationship with music and has used it, or at least sound in various forms to expand, enhance and elaborate upon a whole range of activities.

These activities have normally found expression in worship and ceremonials of some kind where someone, or something, was recognised as being of importance and deserving of special attention. Traditionally this was done in a variety of ways, through words expressed in the form of eulogies for example, or chants designed to catch and focus the attention of those present on what was actually happening. This also includes acts that could be described as 'magickal' which is how the term to '*en-chant*' originates. In fact anything that would serve to make the point and allow the celebrants to participate more fully in what was happening.

The Solfeggio Frequencies
The Church used to employ these techniques on a regular basis, which produced such oddities as the 'Solfeggio Frequencies', said to be entrained in Gregorian Chants (and the tuning of stringed instruments) which, according to the Church, were able to produce feelings of sanctity, well-being and even healing in listeners. This was of course ideal from the point of view of the Church, because it served to get its message more deeply entrenched into the individual psyches of its flock. The frequencies consist of nine specific notes and tones (whose values range from 174Hz to 963 Hz) and were apparently derived from the ancient divinatory science of Gematria. That the early Church should employ quasi-magickal, consciousness altering techniques should present no surprises, because religion of all shades,

irrespective of creed, is solidly based on supernatural and magickal foundations. Although most of the mainstream churches are well aware of this, none of them are especially comfortable about discussing it because of the many and far reaching implications.

The Devil's Chord

Setting the Solgeggio Frequencies aside for one moment, from the Church's position these anodyne musical tones had their exact opposite in what came to be called *'The Devils Chord'*, or the *'Diabolus in Musica'*, where other specific frequencies produced quite the opposite effect and induced feelings of unease and disquiet in those who heard them. This 'Devil's Chord', more correctly called a 'tritone' or 'augmented fourth', is produced when the notes F# C and A (the corresponding frequencies are 370Hz, 523Hz, and 880Hz) are played together especially in a building like a church built to a ratio called the 'Golden Mean'. The Golden Mean, also sometimes called the Divine Proportion, is reckoned to be a ratio of 1.618 and is found literally throughout the entire universe, it is a mathematical constant in everything from the shape of a grain of wheat to the curve of galaxies.

It was often, and indeed still is used, by artists and architects to produce designs that have a strange natural harmony and are pleasing to the human eye. It was regularly used in the design of churches and cathedrals and it is this that may have had an unexpected side effect in regard to the Devils Chord. Why this should be the case in far from clear and hints at fundamental truths about the human race and the nature of the universe itself, perhaps this is connected in some way to how the human brain is hard-wired. There is a creeping suspicion that the ancients and their preoccupation and theorising about the ubiquity of number may well have pointed the way for future generations, but as yet that has not occurred as it should and, instead, the strictures and need for order imposed by science have acted as a filter stopping, or at least hindering, further investigation.

Of course there are variations of this, but in those far off and much simpler times the overall effect was that feelings of dissonance and unease were produced and the Church was having none of that. Although perhaps not, because it has also been argued that the frequencies may also have induced certain susceptible members of the congregation while at worship to temporarily enter an altered state of consciousness and even experience a vision, possibly (given the setting) of the 'divine'. This was even more reason that the Church would rule it out; after all at that time it alone decided who got to experience the sacred and supernatural and indeed what was defined as 'sacred' and 'supernatural'.

The result of this was that during the Middle Ages the Church promptly banned the use of this musical interval in all forms (not just in a sacred setting) in the European countries where it held sway, which effectively meant all of Europe as we now know it, and this ban lasted for decades. If anyone is interested, the tone is widely used today in a variety of settings, The Simpson's TV show uses it in the opening sequence as does Deep Purple's 'Smoke on the Water' and Jimi Hendrix also used it regularly in his inspired guitar playing: 'Purple Haze' is a good example.

Another interesting use of sound as it applies to music can be seen in the works of Wagner, where one of his dramatic orchestral pieces was designed to emulate the explosion of a volcano, but for technical reasons this was not possible at the time the score was written. It was only fairly recently in the late 20th century that the score was actually reproduced as originally intended using an orchestra plus large bass speakers being driven at low frequencies from a powerful amplifier. This produced rumbling sensations inside the bodies of the audience as the speakers emulated the frequencies produced during volcanic eruptions, it was reported that some of the audience felt nauseous and dizzy.

It is of course arguable that comparing relatively modern terms like Hz (Hertz) as related to the Solfeggio Frequencies and the Devils Chord proves nothing, since the terms are not concurrent, i.e. the frequencies of Gregorian chants etc and musical tuning predate modern scientific terms of reference by centuries, but this may not necessarily be the case. The fact that we can now pinpoint the causes of ancient techniques using modern technology does not invalidate their effects; besides, the original discovery of these effects was probably accidental anyway, but that is no reason why they would not have been used.

We still see it today in various settings, although as we have seen not necessarily in churches or anything with obvious religions connections. Another common example is the music used to enhance the visual and dramatic impressions in TV drama or, in particular, films. In this example music is used like a kind of psychic cue or cattle prod specifically designed to evoke various emotions in order that the visuals can produce a much deeper and profound effect on the audience, a sort of sensory 'double whammy' to make a point. The simplest illustration of this was the pianists who used to accompany silent films supplying the desired kind of musical background; either tender and romantic or some stirring martial music.

Why should this be of any interest in a magickal sense? Well, in the early days of Rock 'n' Roll, especially in the ultra-conservative Deep South of the United States, music of this kind carried profoundly racist overtones and was routinely associated with blues music, which was of course the type of music favoured by blacks. It was common to see evangelical, fundamentalist, fire and brimstone pastors ranting and preaching damnation at anyone who listened to, or became involved with, music of this kind. Therefore in their estimation rock music was the work of Satan and was to be condemned and forbidden at any and all opportunity.

Of course the simple fact is that without the blues there would be no rock music and never entered into equation, especially since those making the accusations would and could not understand the almost magnetic attraction of the music amongst the young. Likewise they failed to grasp the equally simple expedient that when you ban, or try to ban, something you make it even more desirable; some things never change. This remarkably backward and offensive philosophy has continued almost to the present day and although Christian fundamentalism still flourishes, the more obvious contradictions and stupidities have largely vanished except at the very fringes.

'Backmasking'

However, in the late 1970's and early 80's a new musical foe emerged, and that was the alleged use of 'backmasking' on some of the tracks created by several bands from the 'heavy metal/death metal' strand of rock music. It has to be said that some of these bands assiduously courted controversy and played up to their supposed occult connections and philosophy. Iron Maiden worked at this connection, as did Judas Priest and Black Sabbath, but other than the graphic, dark imagery the stage shows used, there was no full-on occult connection and even less with the technique of 'Backmasking' .There were some Norwegian bands (in fact the Norwegians and Scandinavians in general almost had a fetish for the more outré ends of rock music: perhaps it's connected with their Viking ancestry) who were almost certainly involved in Satanic and occult practises, but this was co-incidental to their music.

Some bands who actually used the backmasking technique were Slayer, a 'thrash metal' band who used it on their 'Hell Awaits' album, where a deep voice (the unsettling type normally associated with dramatised demonic voices e.g. as used in the iconic and profoundly troubling film, The Exorcist) can be heard repeatedly saying *'Join us'*. Another metal band, 'Cradle of Filth' who were noted for the Satanic imagery, used a reversed reading of The Lords Prayer on a track called 'Dinner at Deviant's Palace'. The use of The Lords Prayer in this manner is a standard feature of the Black Mass; so was this used for genuinely Satanic proposes or, as the band claims, just effect? Make of it what you will.

Some other better known, almost mainstream bands who did use the technique in their music (although not for any overtly magickal purpose) were Led Zeppelin in 'Stairway to Heaven'. The Beatles used it in the track 'Revolution 9' on 'The White Album' and by coincidence at one point in their career in the 1970's there was a widely spread rumour that Paul McCartney had been killed and replaced by a talented double, mention of this was supposedly encoded into another track on one of their albums. Another reference was supposed to be the iconic image taken of the band on a zebra crossing in Abbey Road where Paul is barefoot and out of step with the other members of the band. This crossing has attained a considerable cult status and can been seen online in real time 24/7 via a live feed from a webcam.

Pink Floyd also dabbled with backmasking in a track on 'The Wall' album and the unforgettable band Queen supposedly used it on the track 'Another One Bites The Dust'. However, the most famous; or perhaps that should be infamous, usage was the case of Judas Priest and involved the suicide in 1985 of one youth, Raymond Belknap and the attempted suicide of another, James Vance, after listening to their music for several hours. This tragedy took place after the young men had imbibed a considerable amount of beer and smoked a quantity of marijuana while listening to the track *'Better By You, Better Than Me'*.

According to Vance who survived after blowing off half his face with a shotgun (he died in a coma three years later), they both went to a school playground with a 12-bore shotgun where Belknap shot himself dead and Vance survived, although he was badly wounded both physically and mentally by the experience. In the technique of audio backmasking, words and sounds are encoded into the recording but, as the name suggests backwards, and during replay the words can be heard and by some process, possibly subliminally (perhaps the correct term should be 'sub-audibly') the brain hears them and turns them round. This supposedly produces a kind of post-hypnotic reaction and in a strange parallel with 'electronic telepathy' the person who hears it presumably does or thinks something in response to this.

The parents of the two youths successfully filed charges against Judas Priest claiming that if played backwards, the track contained the words, *'Do it'*, and the band were put on trial. This came about because the survivor said that he had made a suicide pact with his friend and felt that he has no choice other than to obey and they had somehow been programmed by the track. The case came to trial and (much to the relief of all the interested parties in the record industry) was thrown out through lack of either proof or evidence. If this has gone through and any form of culpability had been established can you imagine the floodgates of claim and counterclaim that would have opened in a notoriously litigious country like the USA?

Two of those credited for drawing the attention of the public to the use of Satanic backmasking are Pastor Gary Greenwald and the Rev Jacob Aranza who fulminated long and hard about the corruption of American youth through the use of Satanic backmasking in music and condemned the bands who they claimed were responsible. Rev Aranza even produced a book about it called *'Backward Masking Unmasked'* where he really drove the point home. It has to be stressed that even on the fundamentalist Christian fringe where individuals like Pastors Aranza and Greenwald operate; they only spoke for a few people. Actually if one steps back and looks at the situation they were actually trying to substitute one form of control (Satanic) for another (Christian), not all that different from what the medieval Church was doing. At any rate, after the panic of the 70's and 80's the furore eventually ceased and although the technique is still used, it is (hopefully) purely for effect.

The Use of Subliminals

There is one relatively well-known way in which techniques like this have been used commercially, usually in behaviour modification to help someone stop smoking, or overcome shyness or perhaps in weight loss. Here the commands are recorded on, e.g. a cassette tape and played back in a recorder set to a very low volume level and placed under the pillow of the person undergoing treatment. The commands and instructions are heard by the person while asleep and become imprinted into their subconscious minds and this is supposed to modify what they do and perhaps it does. The truth of the matter is that, according to some experts, the use of backmasking is not an effective way of getting a covert message across, although there are many who would disagree, but that leads on to other areas where the public is deliberately and unknowingly manipulated.

If looked at rationally it is easy to find links between backmasking and other forms of 'information coding', such as the use of subliminal messages in films, especially where advertisers tried to promote different goods during the performances. Although it is officially banned in advertising, the technique was in fact been used in filmmaking and the aforementioned all-time classic horror film, *'The Exorcist'*, is a prime example of this. There are at least two points during the film when, for the briefest moment, the image of a demonic face can be glimpsed. The director, William Friedkin, claims that these inserts cannot be subliminal if one can see them, but the point is that many people could not (as it happens I could) and they were excised from some later prints of the film.

The film also makes very specific, extremely brief and highly effective use of sound as well, (in this case the sound of pigs squealing) and this was incorporated into the film at key points as well. Strangely enough, the Disney studio used to incorporate extremely risqué subliminal images into various cartoons (without the knowledge of the sainted Walt of course) in a display of irreverent humour. There are of course other ways of doing the same thing that are absolutely obvious and in no way 'hidden', other than being hidden in plain sight. There are many examples of how this is done, but consider that the next time you see a politician visiting a war zone he is invariable depicted standing in front of the uniformed troops so that the viewer at home makes the subconscious link of approval between what the politician says and the troops. The public is continually assaulted by techniques like these on a daily basis in the media by advertisers and more especially by politicians of all hues.

The music industry is also guilty of this type of exploitative advertising (again) and it can be seen with the band *'Dio'* where the name of the band was drawn in such an elaborate way that, if inverted, it formed the word 'Devil'. This was not accidental and it appears to show that for those who promote some rock bands, the occult and demonic still presumably has a perceived attraction for their target audience. In fact when the band Genesis was originally formed there was a great fuss made and those who were promoting the band asked the Church of England if any offence would be taken; the Church wisely said *'No'*.

In truth, the public is continually manipulated in a variety of ways, particularly in the manner in which supermarkets are laid out, the flat-pack universe of the furniture retailer IKEA is a notable offender. This company uses a remarkable formula designed to disorientate the people (its customers) who pass through its doors. This is called the *'Gruen Transfer'* and is named after an Austrian architect named Victor Gruen and deliberately configures the layout and colour schemes to disorientate, confuse and partly make the customer forget why they originally decided to pay a visit to the store. If you think that any given supermarket is laid out on a random manner think again, for they are not, they are laid out specifically to induce you to spend money and they are very good at it too, it is why in many cases we 'impulse buy' an article. All part and parcel of helping you lose focus on why you came in to start with, is this a kind of magick? Well, depending on how one looks at it when messing around with perception I suppose it is,

From what we have seen there is little doubt that various highly dubious and borderline ethical techniques have been used, mainly in a covert fashion, to convey messages for various purposes. As far as their use to promote an overtly Satanic agenda goes, whether this was done (because done it certainly was), with a genuinely magickal intent is dubious, but of course quite possible, but it is more likely to have been designed to attract attention and if it did to that extent it can be deemed a success. As for the rest, well we live in a world that is the product of advertising agencies, all of which are staffed by a new breed of magician and sleight of hand merchant. Perhaps being forewarned may help us in knowing what is happening and allow us to make better judgements, but perhaps this article is part of the same campaign: you have been warned!

Chapter Ten
Get Thee Behind Me Satan: Demonic Possession and Exorcism

There are a few categories of paranormal and supernatural phenomena that are almost too terrifying to contemplate. One is how poltergeists manifest and the other, depending on one's religious outlook, is even worse and that is the possession of a human being by an evil spirit or demon. This second example, again depending on whether one is religious or not, helps focus and define belief, because if there is such a thing as demonic (and/or satanic) possession, the logically there should also be a creator God. This if nothing else demonstrates the laws of balance in the cosmos, high and low, salt and sweet good and evil…and the ultimate Gnostic truth: *'As above, so below'.*

It also implies that if both ends of this particular spectrum do exist then, traditionally the 'good' i.e. 'God' should be able to vanquish the bad, i.e. Satan or one of his lieutenants. The why's and wherefores of this, although obviously important, are not the subject of this chapter, but are based around the supposition that if God made the cosmos (and by extension Satan), then He has the final say over who or what is allowed to happen in it and in which order. Unfortunately it does not explain why possessions occur in the first place, but this tends to be attributed to the inherent weakness and fallibility of human beings and the assumption that Satan is constantly seeking out those who he can subsume and control.

The reason that I do not intend to get mired in the theology of all this is because it is long, complex and as with the previous chapter based entirely on faith alone. However theology or not, it does appear that demonic possession, or something very like it, can and does occur and there are several classic literary examples of this One of the most famous is the notorious incident in medieval France that was dramatised by Aldous Huxley in his 1952 book *'The Devils of Loudon'*. The book was later filmed in 1972 by Ken Russell as *'The Devils',* and is a film that in its unflinching portrayal of the savagery employed by religious orders, still to this very day has the ability to shock. We shall come across this again a little later with the incidents that served as the background to the all time standout genre film 'The Exorcist'. However, unlike the events depicted in the in back story to The Exorcist, two other famous exorcisms described here, including the events in Loudon, may have had other more pragmatic origins and purposes.

The Loudon Exorcism

The events described at Loudon in these materialistic and rationalist times are presented, not as demonic possession, but as a secular mixture of religious hysteria, obsession and sexual repression combined with a personal vendetta. All of this effectively resulted in the state sanctioned torture and eventual immolation of a priest, Urbain Grandier. However, there may have been much more to it than that and the case is also believed to be one of the most prolific examples of demonic possession ever recorded. As we will see, the whole thing may indeed have been a charade, an elaborate and protracted act of revenge, or, on the other hand, there may equally well have been a genuinely terrifying supernatural element to it

Urbain Grandier, who was born in 1590 into a fairly wealthy family with political connections, served as parish priest in the French town of Loudon in the diocese of Poitiers. In addition to being something of a free sprit, he chose to largely ignore his vow of celibacy and openly conducted affairs with at least two local women. Unfortunately for Grandier, though their fathers both of the women had links to the Royal Court and these libidinous exploits indirectly led to his downfall. In openly flaunting the rules of celibacy he caused considerable outrage and open hostility (or perhaps jealousy might be more appropriate) among the Catholic hierarchy of the area and in 1630 he was arrested on charges of immorality.

It was at this point that, much to his relief, his political connections saved him and he was discharged and restored to his position as parish priest. Grandier's main adversary, the Bishop of Poitiers, had presided over the proceedings while he stood trial and made no secret of the fact that he wanted him out of his diocese. What happened next is something of a mystery and there are two versions of what happened, although either way Grandier was put to death at the stake.

In the first version of events it is speculated that given the manner in which those suspected of sorcery or witchcraft were treated, the Bishop of Poitiers approached the confessor to the local convent of Ursuline nuns, a Father Mignon, and asked him to persuade the Mother superior 'Jeanne des Anges' (or 'Sister Jeanne of the Angels') to help him. At any rate Father Mignon approached the Mother Superior who agreed to say that Fr Grandier had bewitched her, causing her to take fits and fall to the ground writhing, cursing, using the most appalling profanities and 'speaking in tongues'.

It is not too unusual that in this case speaking in tongues (a phenomenon now referred to as 'glossolalia') was used to indicate possession by some malign entity, because in modern times at least, Pentecostalists and other evangelicals still claim this is a sure sign that those so affected have been chosen as a channel for the Holy Spirit. Obviously at the time of the Loudon Possessions this was not the case and because the circumstances were different such displays were assumed to be demonic. It should be realised that the existence of demons and other evil spirits, especially during this especially superstitious era, was accepted absolutely without question as was the literal truth of scripture, so small wonder that sorcery was also so readily accepted. This is as it applies to Evangelical 'deliverance ministry' which, although the outcome can be similar, is by no means the same as Church sanctioned exorcism.

The other version of events suggests that Sister Jeanne had already heard about the sexual exploits of Grandier and having had some contact with him during pastoral visits to the convent, found him extremely attractive and developed an obsession about him. In a direct parallel with the demonic Incubus, this caused her to dream about Grandier in the guise of a 'bright angel' who came to her in the night and persuaded her to have sex with him. This caused her to cry out in her sleep, which the other nuns could hear. The Mother Superior was horrified at these overtly sexual dreams and the illicit pleasure she obtained from them and performed drastic penances upon herself including flagellation to cleanse the taint of perceived sin. She then discovered that other nuns in the convent were having similar dreams, so she sent for their confessor, Father Mignon, to exorcise the convent of 'demons'. Mortification of the flesh was (and in many cases still is), a regular device employed to indicate great piety and sanctity. This could also be interpreted as the old dictum of doing what you like as long as you don't enjoy it and also finds resonance with the practises of religious ascetics who used to punish themselves horribly to show sympathy for the suffering of Christ on the cross.

Whatever the cause of the disturbances in the convent and despite all the political machinations in the background, the unfortunate Grandier was eventually accused of sorcery and arraigned before the local Inquisition and asked to explain himself. This resulted in him being put, not only to 'the question', but to 'the extraordinary question'. The difference between these related forms of interrogation was quite simple; if put to 'the question' an admission of guilt by the accused brought the hideous torture to an end.

However an admission of guilt when being asked 'the extraordinary question' did not stop the agony, which continued until the inquisitor had piously decided it was over. In any event Grandier, whose legs had been broken during his torture, at no point implicated anyone else or recanted his original story. All to no avail of course and he was found guilty and when due to be burned he had to drag himself to the stake on the shattered remains of his legs. He was not even given the mercy of strangulation before burning either (he had been promised this), but the rope at his neck, probably deliberately, had no slip knot

This demonstration of fervour served as a milestone in the campaign of the Church to confront Satan at every and all opportunities, and despite the fact that modern psychiatrists and psychologists can explain away many of the symptoms displayed by the nuns, there are still some unanswered questions. Records from the time indicate that one of the Church appointed exorcists who took over from Grandier, a Fr Surin, took the invading demons into his body during the ritual and later died insane and screaming in a Jesuit run monastery. One of several other exorcists, a Fr Lactance, was cursed by Grandier as the flames licked round him on the pyre and obligingly died when the unfortunate priest had predicted.

Whatever the eventual outcome, the outbreak of possession in the convent ceased and Satan was apparently sent packing, all of which admirably demonstrated the power of both God and his Church, but with hindsight and removed from the rabid superstition of the era we can make our own judgements. Was the whole thing a trumped up (and costly) affair to rid the church of an inconvenient priest, or was Grandier indeed a closet sorcerer who practised a form of Tantrism and sex magick and his promiscuous activities both in the community and the convent were a part of that? The truth, as always, is written by the victors so we will never know. However there are elements of the case that resonate powerfully with another set of events that occurred, again in France, a few decades earlier.

The Miracle of Luon.

Once again we encounter another apparent possession in medieval France, but this time of a sixteen year old girl, Nicole Obry (sometimes spelled Aubrey) who, according to the legends that surround the case, became possessed by one of the Lords of Hell, none other than Beelzebub Himself. This possession took place in late 1565 when the girl prayed at the grave of her grandfather and according to her account she heard her grandfather speaking to her. The voice asked for a pilgrimage to be done on his behalf to help gain his release from Purgatory. It transpired that this did not happen, which is apparently when the possession began; it has been suggested that her grandfathers' spirit had opened up a 'gateway' for the invading entity. 'Purgatory' is, as the name suggests, a place where souls in a state of grace go to be 'cleansed' or 'purged' of impurity prior to entering Heaven and is a concept that finds direct parallels in all of the monotheistic faiths.

At this point the girl began exhibiting classic signs of possession; screaming, cursing, performing wild physical contortions and speaking in a strange voice; she also refused to eat and quickly became ill. Fearing the worst her parents took her to the local church where demonic possession was promptly diagnosed. The family engaged the services of Dominican monk, Pierre de la Motte, who apparently succeeded in exorcising several demons who, according to the records, immediately departed for Geneva. The main possessor, who identified itself as *'Beelzebub, the prince of the Huguenots'* remained (more of this Huguenot connection later). This demon refused to leave unless the Bishop was sent for and personally conducted the exorcism. The bishop was sent for and duly arrived and after a futile initial attempt at exorcism in the church, had Nicole transferred to the cathedral where, after saying a Mass, he applied himself (along with helpers) to the lengthy and onerous task of driving out the demon.

It is worth stopping to consider that along with many of the 'old gods' attached to the beliefs that had preceded Christianity, entities such as Baal, who in Christian demonology is one of the Seven Princes of Hell (the name Baal means 'master' or 'lord') were co-opted to serve as the bogeymen against whom God battled for the very soul of humanity. I suppose one could, using the modern analogy adopted during the occupation of a territory by the victors following a battle, regard this as a kind of 'hearts and minds' operation. In that respect the exorcism of such a powerful entity was quite a feather in the cap of whoever could achieve it

To this end the exorcism, like the one years later at Loudon, attracted thousands of thrill seekers and a scaffolding and stage were constructed in order to allow the curious a better view of the proceedings. From the existing accounts what occurred was suitably dramatic, colourful, occasionally extreme and lasted for around two months all told. The girl displayed feats of great strength and her face became inflated like a bladder; her tongue also protruded grotesquely from her mouth. She displayed wild contortions where she bent herself backwards so that her heels touched the back of her head. In addition various conversations between 'Beelzebub' and the bishop took place with the demon asserting that he was there to convince the faithful of the attractions of rejecting the Catholic faith to become Huguenots.

The end came after Bishop de Bours started feeding the girl with communion wafers and consecrated wine, which produced an example of levitation where Nicole was raised some distance (six feet according to the records) above the trestle on which she lay. Seeing this, the assembled faithful redoubled their prayers to God to assist the bishop in his endeavours. Further proof of the possession was shown by allowing selected members of the crowd to touch the girl and even stick pins in her feet to show that she felt no pain. A variant on this was seen during the craze for witch persecutions when 'devils marks' were discovered by pricking the poor wretches with bodkins until a numb spot, impervious to pain, was discovered. In nearly all cases the bodkin was rigged so that the needle retracted into the handle to fake the effect.

The levitation marked the gradual banishment of the invading demon, until at 3pm on the 8th of February amidst much shrieking, Beelzebub finally left the body of Nicole. This event was witnessed by the assembled throng who gave thanks to the Bishop and God for this display of spiritual strength. Nicole was reunited with her family and husband (she was married) and there the matter should have rested, but it did not. There are some reports that some years later Nicole once again displayed signs of what might or might not have been another possession when she went temporally blind and experienced fits. This time there was no fuss about it and the symptoms gradually vanished of their own accord. The date of the original successful exorcism was celebrated annually, but ended (along with much else) after the French revolution.

The Exorcism of Douglas Deens

The last and probably the best known example of exorcism is extremely effectively portrayed in the iconic film mentioned at the beginning, 'The Exorcist'. It is informative to learn that the former chief exorcist of the Vatican, Fr Gabriele Amorth. Fr Amorth regards this film as a first class example of what demonic possession is and how exorcism works and has suggested that it be used as part of the training of Church exorcists. The case on which it is based is also very probably, unlike the examples already mentioned, a case of genuine possession. In 1949 a young American boy, Douglas Deen (also and confusingly known as 'Robbie'), interestingly enough the family were not Catholic.

The symptoms afflicting 'Robbie', which included loud noises, furniture moving around, his bed shaking etc, lasted for several months and persisted through at least two official Catholic Church exorcisms. They were only resolved when, with the family's permission, the boy was eventually baptised into the Catholic Church. On the 18th of April 1949, after enduring four months of possession, Robbie was exorcised in a hospital run by the order of Alexian

Brothers. During the ritual a loud cracking noise that resounded through the hospital was heard and the entity abruptly departed, evidently Robbie was finally and permanently 'cured'.

The reason why the entity should have decided to 'occupy' this young boy appears to have been his repeated use of the Ouija board. By using this device which is designed to contact the spirits of the dead, the boy had unwittingly opened a gateway between the dimensions allowing the invading entity through to take possession of him. Some of these entities, whether infernal or not are, according various accounts, entirely inimical to humanity in general and continually seek ways to attack us. It is also suggested that it is not the 'soul' that they desire, but instead they act as *'psychic leaches'*, feasting on the negative emotions and fear their presence generates in human beings. Whether they are the psychic remnants of the dead is an entirely different question and one to which there is no easy or ready answer.

Deliverance Ministry

Perhaps surprisingly in these supposedly enlightened times there are groups of charismatic and evangelical Christians who are, like their medieval forefathers, convinced that just about everything that ails human beings is demonic or satanic in nature. To this end they organise rallies and gatherings of like minded people to come along and receive the blessings of God and in the course of this have invading demons driven out. These demonstrations are, to say the least, dramatic and not a little alarming. Unfortunately, although many of those who organise these evangelical crusades are no doubt sincere they may also be deluded, but their absolute and unswerving faith does not, and perhaps cannot, allow them to see it like that.

Now, that is just the pastors, preachers, evangelists and self-styled 'exorcists'; but the people who attend these meetings and are supposed to be 'possessed' are something else again. In fact it is likely that those who participate in this style of religion are in an almost symbiotic relationship with those who preach it, they feed off one another. The evangelists whip themselves into a froth of righteousness and the congregation, (or at least some of them), became convinced that they are in fact possessed when all that is happening is that they are becoming increasingly confused, afraid, frantic and hysterical in their desire to please the preacher and be seen to be 'cleansed'.

The outcome of this is that the evangelist calls on the demons to come forward and obligingly they do, albeit reluctantly. Demons of lust, of hatred, of fear, of laziness, of headaches of illness and even sore stomachs. Demons of sleepiness, of suspicion and pretty much anything else you can think of is, according to these weird beliefs, attributable to demonic infection. Anyway, as the demons come forth the sufferer throws themselves to the ground writhing and screaming and frothing at the mouth. The evangelist/exorcist then approaches and engages the demons in conversation attempting to drive them out, it is not uncommon for literally dozens of demons to emerge from one person as they writhe, scream and frequently vomit.

Regarding the events that occurred at Luon and Loudon, we should keep in mind that in these two examples of supposed demonic possession and exorcism, there were back-stories that are not generally acknowledged. As we saw at Luon there was repeated mention of the Huguenots (especially from Beelzebub who announced that he was their prince) during the exorcism. The

Catholic Church was fighting a battle to retain its grip (and therefore power and influence) over the population and anything that threatened this had to be resisted at all costs. Why else should the supposed demon announce that it was a Huguenot and why should the demons that had been expelled set off for Geneva? Geneva was of course a centre of the Protestant faith.

In fact, during the exchanges between the Bishop and 'Beelzebub' the demon stated that the Huguenots were evil and desecrated communion wafers, this may seen inconsequential to us, but at that time it was an extremely serious crime. The entity continued on this line by stating that the Huguenots would do more harm to Christ than the Jews had done. Obviously the Church could settle several scores here: show conclusively that it had God on its side by driving out Satanic entities and at the same time demonstrate that the Huguenots were in league with the devil. The turbulent times in which all this happened has to be kept firmly in mind when judging whether or not there ever was any demonic possession at all, or the whole thing was entirely stage managed and orchestrated by the Church

The Loudon affair also had aspects that might raise some suspicions, the antipathy and open hostility felt towards Urbain Grandier by his superiors being the main one. In addition to that was the possibility that the accusations levelled at the unfortunate priest might well have been occasioned by the ravings of a woman fixated and infatuated by him, but whose repressed sexual urges were unfulfilled. It is known that hysteria can and does have many unexpected and dramatic side effects on those affected, especially in cases of religious hysteria. Events related to various forms of hysteria have been recorded in other convents and prisons both male and female so the effects are very real and can manifest in many surprising ways.

However, there are still aspects of both cases that leave a measure of doubt, but in the comparatively recent of 'Robbie' there was no obvious axe to grind or need for point scoring by any of those involved. This appears to be what it claimed to be; a genuine case of possession by 'something' that was eventually forced to leave the body of the youngster involved. Again there are many questions to be asked, particularly what actually does the possessing? How does 'it' get in and why is one particular person selected? Is the entire body possessed or just the brain? This would appear to be the best guess here, because if the mind controls the body once that has been successfully overpowered the rest would be relatively easy. Of course this would not and cannot explain many of the manifestations like the alleged levitations and the spontaneous movement of items of furniture and ornaments etc. Then there are the loud and spontaneous noises so typical of poltergeist manifestations and the anomalous voices as well.

Phenomena like levitation has also been attributed to many saints, i.e. St Theresa of Avilla and St Thomas of Cupertino, surely nothing demonic here, so what is occurring? Certainly a demonstration of some unknown but powerful force at work, but originating where; in the body of the person afflicted or an external source? It is a pity that it no longer seems to occur, or if it does it is not reported because we could learn so much, although given the nature of the scientific establishment it would sooner sideline and ignore such inconvenient events. On the other hand there is one branch of research that probably would, for obvious reasons, embrace such knowledge and that would be whatever branch of the defence and/or the intelligence community that could find a use for it, as they undoubtedly would.

The Hutchison Effect

Nothing is set in stone, especially in the wake of current research into paranormal phenomena and the following observations comments about something called The Hutchison Effect stem from background research I carried out some years ago and was based on the evidence then available. My views have since changed, but nonetheless some of the concepts expressed here are still viable and strongly held by researchers whose ideas are rooted in the purely spiritual. It is modern twist on what has been discussed in this chapter and it involves an extremely enigmatic phenomenon called 'The Hutchison Effect' (HE) which has been linked to displays of apparent poltergeist activity.

This 'effect' is where the odd and anomalous effects allegedly caused by electromagnetic fields were monitored both overtly and covertly by the US (and other) intelligence services. It was no accident that this all occurred at around the time when such covert operations as the 'Stargate Project' were also being evaluated. It was a period when just about anything went and any and all types of borderline phenomena were studied and evaluated for possible intelligence and military use. Although his so-called 'effect' is still hotly debated, there is no doubt that the intelligence services were more than a little interested in what it implied, so much so that they still go to remarkable lengths to deny they ever investigated it.

So, what did this curious effect entail? Briefly, a self-funded Canadian electromagnetic researcher John Hutchison had in his laboratory as an adjunct to his research a collection of devices that emit localised strong electromagnetic (EM) fields. These included a Van de Graaff generator, Tesla Coils, RF generators and other bits and pieces of electronic equipment that would produce an EM) field as part of their normal operation. Hutchison observed with astonishment that a by-product of all this equipment was the apparent production of intermodulating EM fields of various strengths. In turn these fields appeared to produce the spontaneous movement of various items lying around the lab, later designated by Hutchison as *'hot spots'*. Small and large, light and heavy, ferrous and non-ferrous, these items lifted and moved around while his collection of electrical equipment was switched on.

Not only that, orbs of lights appeared in the air and metal distorted, and all at standard household voltages, (in this case Canadian) of 110v AC at 60Hz. According to my information the maximum load did not exceed 1.5 kW, which is less than that of an average domestic heater or cooker. Given the relatively low power usage the results obtained are remarkable. In addition, small fires started spontaneously in various parts of the building some distance from the site of the experiment. This would seem to indicate that the effect is not necessarily confined to the immediate vicinity of the source of the radiation and it is important to understand that.

Like 'conventional' poltergeist activity, the occurrences were random, pointless and often days apart. I have no doubt that this happened and I have seen a copy of videotape taken by Hutchison showing a variety of the apparently random activity as it occurred within his laboratory. I doubt the sincerity of either John Hutchison or the English researcher Mr Albert

Budden, who introduced the news of what Hutchison had discovered to a wide audience and Mr. Budden's obvious interest in and enthusiasm for the concept was the main factor in introducing the information into the UK. Is it not possible that rather than creating the various phenomena by reason of the emission of EM radiation, the device is acting as a receiver or amplifier for external radiation? To quote from an article called, 'The Poltergeist Machine' written by Albert Budden, *"He wonders if somehow the fabric of space-time is actually breached"*.

This was almost a chicken and egg situation, is the Hutchison device broaching the local space-time continuum and allowing 'wild' energies through, or is the device radiating energies of its own creation? While experimenting with the device, an electrical engineer George Hathaway, an assessor acting for the Los Alamos National Laboratory, monitored the ambient EM field strength. This evidently varied between 100,000 and 500,000 uV (microvolts). To bring this into perspective, 500,000 uV equals one half of one volt. It seems to me that this is not a great deal of energy in comparison to the dynamic energy required to move an object weighing (in at least one instance) several kilograms, so in my opinion there has to be some other factor, a form of amplification, direction and control.

It should also be said that the enigmatic Col John Alexander was also deeply involved with what Hutchison said he had discovered in relation to this curious effect. In fact Col Alexander played a considerable role in this and similar projects in his position as a staff officer with the U.S. Army Intelligence and Security Command (INSCOM) where he had the title of 'Chief of Advanced Human Technology', although just what that means is far from certain. He was also, given his ISCOM remit, involved with the Stargate remote viewing project (as in 'The Men Who Stare at Goats') attempted by the US military in recent years.

Although the implication is that the phenomenon is purely electromagnetic in nature, unfortunately I cannot fully accept the rationale behind this conclusion, because there occasionally seems to be an element of intelligence at work behind the manifestations. For example: the apparent interaction between the manifestation and the people affected i.e. producing a demonstration on demand. This I believe is an unwitting example of the 'control' at work. It is possible that there is, under a specific set of circumstances, a direct interaction between emissions from the human brain, which is a source of, - admittedly very weak – electrical emission and the various 'energies' around us. Given that the human brain is a source of low-level electrical energy anyway and can be affected by external electromagnetic radiation, it is in effect both transmitter and receiver.

This then may well be a factor in what produces the conversion of one form of energy to another. I believe that this 'control mechanism' is latent in all of us, especially where there is a great deal of trauma, whether this is from an adult or a young person. In the case of a young person there appears to be a random 'lashing out' of this energy probably due to lack of focus and control, this could well be a by-product of hormonal imbalance. In the case of adults, the physiological changes in body chemistry and the inadvertent triggering of specific synapses brought on by continuous emotional trauma may produce the same effect.

Admittedly, there is an alternative train of thought directly connected to the electromagnetic phenomenon of the Hutchison Effect. The conservation of energy does not apply to poltergeist phenomena or the Hutchison Effect because they are not closed loops. In other words the conversion of thermal energy into kinetic energy would not apply; rather the intermodulation of the EM fields produces the effects when a suitable catalyst is applied, in this case by someone or something that can interact with the field. For example, the phenomena in Hutchison's lab did not occur unless he was present, so, in some manner he had himself become sensitised to the EM radiation and was acting as an organic component.

The condition is known as electromagnetic hypersensitivity (EH), something else popularised by Albert Budden, and appears to occur when magnetite within the human body becomes 'charged' through prolonged exposure to EM radiation. This presents one, but by no means the only, method of 'control' over the bizarre effects created by the EM fields. It is important to remember that this sensitisation is possible in human beings due to various levels of magnetite in the human body that in certain circumstances can and does become magnetically charged.

One particularly disturbing aspect to the subject is the apparent interest shown by various governments to this phenomenon. Hutchison approached both the US and Canadian governments. The US army sent a team to examine the events in Hutchison's lab where they took videotapes and made various measurements of field strengths. They later refused to give Hutchison a copy of the report; it had suddenly become 'classified'. The Canadian government did the same, saying it infringed national security: just what has this researcher stumbled on? What arcane military research has been breached here? Given the type of results he obtained there are several intriguing possibilities. Exotic propulsion systems and beam weapons are an example.

It is regrettable that this section is peppered with 'perhaps' and 'maybe', but as I said these comments are based on matter is open to various explanations, and I do not necessarily subscribe to the spiritual aspect, because there may be a more rational, albeit unusual, physical explanation. There are also several unanswered questions, e.g. has any serious attempt been made to replicate the experiment? I am inclined to believe, based on personal experience, that the phenomenon is connected to the propagation of electromagnetic radiation within a specific band-width. I also believe there is an element of 'control' involved, probably from interaction with a human agency. Perhaps the answer is in this rather free (mis) quote from the late pioneering researcher and inventor of AC motors Nicola Tesla, when asked by an admirer if there was any fundamental truth behind various phenomena, in effect a theory of everything, Tesla said "Resonance, vibration and frequency". Who knows, it's as good an explanation as any.

My own investigations and enquiries into this phenomenon eventually bore fruit when I finally contacted the Los Alamos National Laboratory (LANL) in Albuquerque, New Mexico, who were responsible for the initial evaluation of the HE at the behest of the US Intelligence services; they denied all knowledge until I presented them with the proof. Questions, speculation and yet more questions, but sadly there are no conclusive answers to many of these events and what information did emerge should be viewed entirely on its own merits, but the one thing that shines through is this. As long as we have the desire to explore the secrets of the human condition and learn then the impossible eventually becomes possible and the unknown known; we only need patience, self belief and curiosity.

Chapter Eleven
Slayers! The Last Vampire Hunters

Tales of vampires and their familiars have now become so embedded in our culture, especially in recent times, that it can be difficult to separate fact from fantasy and sometimes sheer wishful thinking. There is no doubt that the vampire has evolved into something considerably more than an enigmatic shape changer with demonic associations, instead, this often terrifying blood drinking immortal has become the very epitome of raffish sophistication and 'cool'. The sybaritic lifestyle of the vampire has become a byword for all that is sensuous, hedonistic and even romantic. The only downside to this is that in order to achieve such a nirvanic state one has, unfortunately, to be dead…or undead to be absolutely correct and from traditional accounts the transformation process is not exactly pleasant. All of this is in direct opposition to the image of that other iconic shape changer and traditional foe of the vampire: the werewolf; but that is another tale for another day.

Although shape changers have millennia long histories in folklore, especially in shamanic traditions, the modern image of the vampire first appeared in the early 19th century from a short story written by Dr John Polidori entitled 'The Vampyre'. The tale centred round a supernatural aristocratic fiend who, in order to survive, consumed the blood of his peers. This struck a resonant chord in the psyche of the general public and morphed into other similar creatures starting with Bram Stoker's long lived, much imitated, but never equalled Dracula and also into generic offshoots like Count Orlok in another classic film of the oeuvre, 'Nosferatu'.

However the only one that actually stayed the course and fired the imagination was the aristocratic (and as a rule dictatorial and autocratic) Count Dracula. Quite why this should be, especially now, is not too difficult to work out. Perhaps it has a lot to do with a desire to emulate the lifestyles of the rich and famous with the additional bonus of black magick, plus a smidgeon of sex, immortality, incredible strength and general naughtiness thrown in. A version of all this can be see in two separate but thematically connected film (and book) franchises, i.e. the 'Twilight' series and of course 'Underworld'.

While both of the variant tales effectively highlight the differences between vampires and werewolves, 'Underworld' is by far the more effective, gritty and visceral. For all that and in spite of the obvious links to fiction this has not prevented a thin layer of belief that such creatures really do exist to take root, and not only in traditional homes of the vampires like Transylvania and Romania. In the case of the undead, unholy creatures of the night mentioned here, each had their nemesis in the form of vampire hunters intent on destroying them, charismatic individuals like Abraham van Helsing, and, appropriately, even fictional characters like that found an analogue in the real world

The belief in the reality of vampires and vampire-like creatures even reached the shores of the United Kingdom and this was almost a century after Stokers' fictional Dracula set foot on these shores at Whitby in the North of England. A more concrete and recent example of a belief in the reality of vampires first emerged in the 1960's when a group of people in London, all amateur ghosthunters, began conducting their dubious research in the marvellously atmospheric Highgate Cemetery in London. It has to be said that this decaying and overgrown urban city of the dead has all the necessary credentials to be a ready made location for horror films. In 1969 David Farrant who belonged to such a group wrote an account of spending a night there and according to him had caught sight of a supernatural grey figure, (but significantly not a vampire) and the word soon spread. Shortly after this event several other witnesses came forward with similar tales of ghostly figures drifting around the graveyard: and this is when, as they say, the plot thickens.

Sean Manchester

Following Farrant's announcement a second seeker appeared on the scene, a local man called The Rev. Sean Manchester, who was determined to track down and eliminate this ghostly presence. According to the Rev Manchester this was no ordinary spectre, but was instead a 'Vampire King of the Undead'. According to him, this entity was a medieval, black magick practising minor member of the Romanian nobility, who had been brought into this country in a coffin by some followers during the 1700's.

He had been buried in the area that had since become Highgate Cemetery. Manchester was adamant that the activities of modern Satanists had roused this creature and the only course of action was to locate the body, drive a wooden stake through its heart, behead it and burn the body. This was splendid, lip smacking, meaty stuff and displaying a typically journalistic instinct for sensation, local and national newspapers went into overdrive. A short time later both men stated that they had seen the remains of several foxes in the cemetery, all with their throats torn out and completely drained of blood.

Farrant and Manchester had by now effectively declared a bizarre sort of 'bidding war', with each of them trying to outdo the other with claims of how they intended to permanently remove the perceived menace. Manchester, a former president of the British Occult Society, eventually announced that he would conduct an exorcism on Friday the 13th of March 1970 and in the early evening of that date the location was inundated with hoards of thrill seekers. However what actually occurred next is not 100% clear, nor is it fully independently verifiable. What evidence there is comes from Manchester's own account set out in his book of the affair, The Highgate Vampire', which he wrote in 1991 and his account of what went on can be condensed as follows.

To avoid a police cordon that had been placed around the main cemetery to thwart the crowds that had assembled, Manchester and some associates entered the cemetery covertly via an adjoining graveyard. Once inside and using the talents of a female psychic they located a vault that, the medium said, was the vampire's lair. They repeatedly attempted to force the heavy vault door (which was made of iron) open, but were unable to do so. Not to be thwarted they climbed up on the roof of the tomb and gained entry via ropes lowered through a hole in the roof and once inside found several empty coffins.

Assuming that the occupants of the coffins were otherwise absent and engaged in gruesome pursuits, using one of several traditional anti-vampire techniques they placed cloves of garlic in the coffins and completed the process with a generous sprinkling of holy water. After this they climbed back up the ropes (they must have been very well prepared, not to mention fit) and surreptitiously left the cemetery though the point of entry. According to his book 'The Highgate Vampire', apparently Manchester did return some months later this time during the day and managed to obtain access to the tomb after finally forcing open the main door, but there were no independent witnesses to this event. Whether their efforts were fruitful is not clear, but a few months later the charred remains of a female corpse were discovered a short distance from the vault. It is assumed this was the handiwork of the satanic groups that, to this day, still allegedly use the location for their ceremonies.

It was also at around this time that Manchester's main competition David Farrant was discovered in the cemetery brandishing a crucifix and wooden stake; he was arrested, but when he appeared in court no charges were pressed. Farrant persevered in his attempts at vampire hunting in Highgate Cemetery and for his pains was eventually jailed for desecrating graves and interfering with the dead. The means of dissuading individuals from disinterring human remains is dealt with slightly differently in other areas of the UK, especially in Scotland where there is a legal proscription called the 'Right of Sepulchre' specifically forbidding it.

This legal proscription has been used in places of considerable interest, like Rosslyn Chapel, to prevent legitimate archaeological investigations taking place. While no doubt a laudable and well-meant article of legislation, it is possible that in its application at Rosslyn there may be the added incentive that should nothing of interest actually be concealed within the chapel (like the Holy Grail, the mummified head of Christ, the Baphomet, the Templar Treasure or any of the other mysterious and/or sacred artefacts that have reputedly been concealed there) it might diminish interest and therefore much needed income.

Eventually the increasing and intense rivalry between these two men culminated in rumours of an eagerly anticipated 'magicians duel' that was supposed to take place on Parliament Hill, but, to the dismay of various interested parties it did not materialise. This so called 'magicians duel' must call into questions the motivations and outlook of both men. This proposed duel had all the hallmarks of one that really did take place many years earlier between the iconic ritual magician Aleister Crowley and Samuel Liddell MacGregor Mathers who was a former friend of Crowley and the one time head of the Golden Dawn. This strongly implies that both Farrant and Manchester had (or should have had) a considerable knowledge of the subject. However, given their relative youth it is unlikely that either of them were sufficiently well versed in this highly dangerous art to engage in such a battle, so it is more likely that the announcement was more to do with attention seeking and ego than anything else

Before leaving the actions of Sean Manchester we should perhaps look a little more closely at the man. Manchester, who in addition to his claims about the reality of vampires, also holds the rank of Bishop and Primate of the Ecclesia Apostolica Jesu Christi, or The Apostolic Church of Jesus Christ in Great Britain. This church, whose first bishop was apparently Christ's uncle, Joseph of Arimathea, claims to have been consecrated by none other than Jesus Christ himself and arrived in Britain around AD 36. However, the church is also and better known by the name of 'The Old Catholic Church', and is a schismatic offshoot of the traditional Roman Catholic Church as we know it today. Oddly enough it does have a connection with another self proclaimed vampire hunter and exorcist, the late and some might say notorious, Montague Summers.

Montague Summers

Much has been said about the barbaric excesses of the medieval inquisitors and rightly so, but less is known about those who chose to condemn magick (and witchcraft) in the most graphic terms in more recent and presumably enlightened times. Only the fact that we no longer live trapped in a morass of superstition, ignorance and fear (plus of course a much more enlightened legal system) prevented them from inciting new witch-hunts with al the attendant hysteria, fear and butchery. Nevertheless a few of these malicious zealots were still were around and one such was Augustus Montague Summers. He was born in April 1880, the youngest of seven children of a prosperous banking family in Bristol, England. His early schooling was unremarkable, but he went on to study theology at the prestigious Trinity College located in Cambridge with the intention of becoming a priest in the Church of England.

He continued his training at Lichfield College and in 1908 achieved the minor rank of deacon in the Anglican Church. He did not receive any further promotions in the church, which may have been due to his abiding curiosity about Satanism. However, his interest in the subject and actually practising it were two entirely different things and should have been no impediment, but rumours of his alleged interest in young boys certainly was. He was tried on charges of this nature, but was eventually found not guilty and acquitted. That said, his first published work in 1907, 'Antinous', dealt with the debased subject of pederasty. It seems strange that it is only now that effective legislation is in place to prevent individuals like Summers having any contact with children. It should also be noted that the God 'Antinous' is also referred to as 'The Gay God' and there is currently a 'Temple of Antinous' located in California USA.

Perhaps it reflected the hypocritical and sanctimonious values of his times where many things were swept under the carpet to maintain the public façade of religious respectability and decency. Unfortunately it is also something that still bedevils the Catholic Church to this day and has been highlighted by, at the time of writing, the evidence of an ongoing cover-up by the Church in Ireland during the late 20th century when it evidently put its own reputation before the interests of children abused by its priests in that country. The severity of the issue also forced the then Pope Benedict XIV to issue a letter of public apology.

In 1909 Summers converted to Roman Catholicism and began to adopt the garb and manner of a priest in that religion which, given his theological training and the similarity between the two faiths, would have been relatively easy. It is here that we should look more closely at his actions, because there may be considerably more to this than meets the eye. Yes, he did convert to a form of Catholicism and adopted the extravagant soubriquet of Father Alphonsus Jesus-Mary Augustus Montague Summers, but this conversion was not in the mainstream Catholic Church, it was in the offshoot called 'The Old Catholic Church'. The Old Catholic Church was founded during the 1870's in Germany as a result of the announcement of papal infallibility by the First Vatican Council in 1869-70 and took the name, 'The Union of Utrecht of Old Catholic Churches'. Although it has no formal connection with the Holy See it does maintain contact with and share many of the ideas of the Anglican Communion. Tellingly, among its differences with the Catholic Church is its acceptance of homosexuality as a lifestyle, which at that time was almost unheard of.

The beliefs of the Old Catholic Church differ markedly from the must more conservative Church of Rome in its already mentioned views on homosexuality, the ordination of women priests, which it has done since 1996, and its refusal to condemn artificial contraception preferring instead to leave it up to the individual couple. From this it is not unreasonable to assume that Summers could more easily identify with the liberal attitude to homosexuality and therefore would feel better disposed to a church like this. However he also became a member of a secret society called 'The Order of Chaeronea', which may give a clearer understanding of his motives in joining the Old Catholic Church and of course to the other charges laid against him. George Cecil Ives founded the Order of Chaeronea in 1897 with the intention of promoting homosexuality with a cultural and spiritual ethos, a concept which at that time was anathema to the general public, but now seems to resonate with the teachings of the Temple of Antinous amongst other organisations.

Ives realised that there was little chance of the homosexual lifestyle being even close to acceptable in that era so he decided to cultivate it secretly and in this way create an environment where homosexuals could mix and socialise with less fear of discovery and the consequent possibilities of ruin and probable imprisonment. To this end he invented an elaborate set of rituals and initiations on similar lines to the Freemasons and other quasi-secret organisations that used signs and handshakes. Another thing that also strikes a resonant chord with Freemasonry was the development of a sign-word, in this case, 'AMRRHMO', which finds a close parallel with Masonic term, 'HTWSSSTKS', which is often found stamped on Masonic pennies. HTWSSSTKS, the original meaning of which is supposedly lost, is remembered by the mnemonic, '**H**iram **T**he **W**idows **S**on **S**ent **S**oon **T**o **K**ing **S**olomon' or variants thereof. The meaning of the mnemonic, 'AMRRHMO', is unknown.

The keen interest that Summers apparently had in homosexuality and his possible paedophile inclinations aside, two of the things best known about him were his at the time unique translation of the odious Dominican witch finding manual, the Malleficorum and the publication of his best known work, 'The History of Witchcraft and Demonology'. (1926, reprinted in 1969). This was followed by a succession of works such as 'The Geography of Witchcraft', (1927) 'A Popular History of Witchcraft' (1937) and 'Witchcraft and Black Magic' (1946). Summers was absolutely convinced that all witches, black or white, were irredeemably in league with Satan and his narrow definition of witchcraft provided no niceties of distinction between Wiccan's, shamans, pagans and Satanists.

As far as he was concerned they were one and the same thing and thoroughly deserved everything coming to them and he was especially enthusiastic about the horrors of the Inquisition. Some, probably apocryphal, stories have hinted that he had a remit from a shadowy organisation within the Catholic hierarchy to seek out, expose and excoriate witchcraft at every opportunity, which of course he did, although this was almost certainly entirely of his own volition. Summers wrote that witches embodied every foul and perverse passion known to man, that were the epitome of evil, they were 'poisoners, worshipers of Satan, blasphemers, rapists, charlatans, bawds and abortionists'.
He cultivated an air of mystery about himself and in appearance Summers was never less than striking and frequently walked around wearing a cloak with his long silvery hair worn almost like a wig, while his fingers gleamed with his many jewelled rings. Oddly enough he did not adopt clerical garb on a regular basis and when he did it was apparently purely for effect. In spite of his short stature he was remarkably charismatic and people who met him were frequently in awe, something that he always used to his advantage. The former wartime member of the British intelligence service and author of many novels on black magick, Dennis Wheatly, said quite categorically that Summers *'Inspired him with fear'*.

It has been suggested that Wheatly based one of his characters, Canon Copley-Style, in his extremely influential and alarming work, 'The Devil Rides Out', on Summers. In addition to his self-appointed role as an implacable foe of witchcraft and other perceived evil doings, in common with Sean Manchester, Montague Summers also developed a keen interest in vampires and werewolves and espoused an unshakable belief in both of these legendary creatures. He went on to produce three books devoted to them, 'The Vampire, His Kith and Kin' (1928), 'The Vampire in Europe' (1929) and 'The Werewolf' (1933).

Because his calling and the era in which he lived, in the course of his occult researches it was almost inevitable that Summers should come into contact with the legendary occultist Aleister Crowley, which he did and against all expectations both men developed a friendship and mutual respect, meeting regularly to discuss and air their totally different viewpoints. On second glance perhaps it is not so surprising after all, since both of them were equally capable of plumbing the depths of the pit in their studies, both were extremely knowledgably in their respective fields and both had strange sexual proclivities. In addition, it is a fair bet that both men had grossly inflated egos and these meetings would probably allow them to preen and demonstrate their knowledge. This same ego driven vanity is also why both enjoyed and deliberately cultivated a high public profile. It should come as no surprise to learn that at one point Aleister Crowley attempted to set up his own religion using the title of 'Crowleyanity'.

Right until he died in August 1948, the year after Crowley, Summers continued his vehement denunciation of magick and witchcraft while promoting the magickal beliefs of his church. He never faltered in his open admiration for the Inquisition and stoutly defended their record of brutality, murder and oppression, it was, after all, carried out with the best of intentions and sanctified in the name of God There can be little doubt that had Summers been born a few centuries earlier, he would have equalled and even surpassed the efforts of such arch-Inquisitors as Dominic de Guzman and Tomas de Torquemada in his efforts to cleanse the planet from his narrow interpretation of sin. Thankfully he was not. As a last and possibly not too surprising observation about Summers, there were suggestions that on December the 24th 1918 he conducted a Black Mass assisted by two young men. This assertion, if true, shows the man as either a dedicated researcher seeking to discover whether magick of this kind actually did produce results, or for the hypocritical pederast that he really was.

So there we have it, two men convinced of their mission to remove vampires, whether real or not, from the face of the earth. .However might they just have been on to something? Without wishing to delve too deeply into a real nest or vipers, it has been suggested that, in line with the rationale behind Chaos Magick certain things, wishes if you like, can be made real by concentrating on them. They are called 'Tulpas' and are a part of the techniques and lore of Tibetan Buddhism. Is if possible that, given the high profile of fictional vampires in our society today, we might actually create one through sheer 'thought pressure'?

The Gorbals Vampire

As a footnote to this, there is a curious parallel between these events and what took place in Glasgow's sprawling and extremely atmospheric Southern Necropolis in September 1954. One evening a local policeman was summoned by concerned locals to a disturbance that had broken in the Necropolis. When he arrived he found dozens of local schoolchildren patrolling the walkways in groups armed with knives, pointed sticks and stones. When asked what they were doing they assured the policeman that they were there to seek out a seven foot tall, steel fanged vampire that had been seen in the vicinity, it had supposedly attacked and killed two children. The alarming tale seems to have escalated from a playground rumour that had got out of hand, but given the sombre nature of the necropolis it is not hard to see why. Might this or something like it be why tales of vampires abounded at Highgate Cemetery? The answer to this is unknown, but perhaps we should start looking closely at some of the reports of strange happenings and sightings in the pages of newspapers, because the truth, as they said in the iconic and long running TV series, 'The X Files', might just be out there.

Chapter Twelve
Before The Beginning

The chapter that follows is based on a mixture of fact, science, observation, information and yes, there is no point in pretending otherwise, a good dollop of speculation, gleaned from what are best defined as 'paranormal' sources, plus just a smidgeon of scripture. It is also a prime example of just how inextricably interlinked many aspects of the paranormal really are. What this chapter also makes very clear is that the subject of paranormal phenomena carries far too much unnecessary and unhelpful baggage with it, especially in how we refer to its many diverse facets. We talk about 'spirits', 'ghosts' and other manifestations of the phenomenon, when what we actually mean is something quite different. It has always seemed reasonable (to me at least) to refer to the 'spirit world' as an alternate reality or even another universe, because that is in effect what it is.

However, since there is no obvious unanimity, consensus or conformity of language on this subject (or indeed what the subject is), we are pretty much stuck with what we have. That said, where appropriate I have tried to use other terms to help demystify the matter. I also wish to express my thanks to Mr Don Philips, the founder of GSI Paranormal, for his invaluable help and assistance in supplying some of the information regarding the hypothetical alternate (but parallel) universe. At this point I should also state unequivocally that I am certain we do continue in another form after physical death. I say this based on two factors, one of which forms part of the laws of thermodynamics, i.e. matter and energy cannot be created or destroyed, but changes in form, added to what I have repeatedly observed and experienced at first hand.

The Scole Group
Some years ago in 1993 a lengthy experiment was begun in the village of Diss in Norfolk, England to establish, or at least attempt to establish, absolute proof of the existence of an afterlife. In other words that physical death is not the end and we do in fact transcend the body and move on to another phase or realm of existence. This was 'The Scole Experiment' and the results appear to prove (although the results as you would expect were and still are hotly disputed by various debunking websites and organisations) that this is indeed the case, and in the course of this lengthy experiment other discoveries were made that, in their way, are every

bit as important as the survival hypotheses and possibly even more so. This is not the first time such an experiment has been attempted and as you will see shortly by no means was it the last; however, one aspect of what occurred in the original experiment is especially interesting and has immense implications.

As part of the lengthy procedure, which was facilitated by Robin and Sandra Foy at a cellar in their home with the assistance of several mediums, plus scrutineers from reputable investigative organisations such as the United Kingdom based Society for Psychical Research (SPR), a fascinating possibility emerged. While a range of contacts were made with those who have passed over from the physical, one aspect of the experiments using blank film stock was particularly interesting and produced a wide spectrum of highly significant results. These included obvious examples of cursive writing and faces, but other images of what looked like varicoloured geometric shapes plus planets suspended in space were also produced. In addition, on one occasion the image of a single entity that looked uncannily similar to the slender 'greys' so synonymous with UFO lore was captured. We shall return to this particular being a little later for it may be crucial in understanding what parallel realities are and how they function.

According to the account, the Scole experimenters were not working alone and had recruited what they called a 'spirit team' who assisted them from the other side; these entities are typical of the denizens that inhabit the various levels of realty existing alongside our own. What makes this team rather different is that after physical death in many cases they apparently carried the skills and abilities they attained while in physical form with them. Some had been technicians while others had been scientists and they were more than willing to use their skills to assist the researchers. This, if true, is also remarkable because as already noted it clearly implies that sentience and intelligence do not abruptly cease with physical death.

In fact, if one thinks about it there is no reason why skills and abilities acquired in the physical state, plus curiosity and the capacity to learn something new, should not remain with anyone who has passed over, the main issue would be how they could be used in a reality that is not physical...or not physical as we understand it. It might imply that the set of parameters that we believe necessary to allow interaction with objects might still be valid, but in a non-physical existence items of equipment might somehow be configured differently at the subatomic level and exist as pure energy that can be interacted with, but that is of course no more than speculation.

As regards the beings that exist in the other realm, many are neither human nor amicable and while some are indeed friendly others are utterly indifferent to us and yet others are implacably hostile to the point where they would do us harm (or worse) should they ever get the chance. This reaction is apparently based on the fact that we as a species possess both form and emotions and are capable of using and expressing them, which apparently is something they cannot do.

Separate Realities and the 'Big Question'.

Setting all that aside for the moment, it is the existence of these alternate realities/worlds in their own right that should really catch our interest. Another highly relevant aspect of this possibility is in the nature of time and how it applies to both the realities and to a lesser extent whatever lives there. I say this because it is often mooted by mediums and psychics that time becomes immaterial after physical death, although like much else associated with spiritual matters this is often hotly disputed. From this notion, quite unbidden, something occurred to me, however it is a question that needs to be examined closely, but the answer, if indeed there is an answer, could have infinitely profound implications for the human race.

The nature of this question was not about surviving physical death, we'll take that as a given, but something perhaps even more far reaching and profound, it was this: *"Did the 'spirit world' exist before the 'Big Bang', or does it owe its existence entirely to the human race"?* This can only be answered in two ways, either it did or it did not and if it did then what kind of entities might have lived there and, more to the point, where did they come from? The equations of one strand of conventional science tell us that prior to the Big Bang there was absolutely nothing; no space, not even the space the singularity that was the universe expanded into and of course no time either. There is another theory that the universe and all it contains has always been here, it is ageless, unchanging and immutable, but this theory is being increasingly discredited so other than acknowledging it as a possibility we shall set that theory to one side

It is far from easy to imagine absolute nothing, no-thing, total non-being, non-existence; it is genuinely terrifying, because our concept of reality is based entirely on there being something tangible, a comforting reality and solidity (including the notion of time) to cling to. These two parameters were created as the minute singularity that was the embryo universe exploding outwards with the cataclysmic fury of a million suns and as far as we know it is still being created as the expansion continues. Difficult as it is to appreciate due to its sheer immensity; at the very boundaries of the universe there is, right now as you read this, *absolutely nothing*, it is the same timeless and formless 'nothing' that existed before the Big Bang until the expanding singularity created reality, just as it did at the beginning. It will continue doing so until the time, many billions of years in the future, that the expansion stops, after that, well, who knows; perhaps a hypothetical 'big crunch' as it all starts to compress once again?

Getting Some Perspective

We now have to once again move inexorably into the realms of speculation here and consider the idea that the paranormal and the concept of alien intelligences are absolutely interlinked. As far as science can estimate the universe is around 13.8 billion years old and the solar system is around 4.6 billion years old and the Earth has been minimally habitable for approx 3 billion years (give or take) and the human race has been around for a tiny fraction of that. By 'human race' I mean *homo sapiens*, i.e. something that we would recognise as a modern human being, has been here for around 200,000 years, which in universal terms is the blink of an eye; no time at all. So, if we were to display our characteristic hubris, it would mean that the 'spirit world' has only existed for the same length of time. However, if there is *no time* associated with this alternate state of existence it would not matter, but it would also mean that from our perspective it cannot have existed until there were 'spirits' to inhabit it and that simply cannot be correct, because we arrive at a sort of existential 'which came first, the chicken or the egg' situation?

If, as we have seen, our solar system is around 4.6 billion years old (we're not even considering the length of time our planet has been habitable) and the universe is much, much older, then the Solar System we live in is a relative 'new kid on the block'. It is highly likely that if civilisations have already come and gone, (as ours eventually surely will) then logically they too must have had their own version of the 'spirit world' and their energy signatures/ spirit must have also traversed the gulf from life to death: or is the ability to have a spirit only part of the human condition? Through the talents of a psychic medium I have spoken to entities that claimed to be non-terrestrial and were able to tap into this alternate universe/spirit world that surrounds us, to all intents and purposes it is the same one, and according to what he/she/it/they said, they too inhabit this continuum after they die.

Apart from anything else, the mere fact that they also die shows that they have a defined lifespan and pass (or perhaps like us that should be 'convert'?) into another state of being. So we return to the question, did the spirit world exist before the Big Bang? And so far we are no further forward, because even although it is also populated by non-human entities and always has been; it is neither clear nor certain what was there before that. For this we have to look for answers elsewhere, in this case from someone called 'Becky' who apparently lives there and to do that we have to introduce GSI Paranormal and Mr Don Philips, but first some background.

Talking to the Departed

In recent times, in the past ten or fifteen years in fact, a strain of ghost hunter (or perhaps 'ghost exploiter' would be a better description, because if spirits are sentient why should we assume they actually want to be contacted?) has emerged and it is a trend that has done this area of research no favours whatsoever. This does not of course detract in any way from the many small, sincere, dedicated groups who set out with a genuine desire to make contact with those who have already made the transition into the alternative existence that awaits us all after physical death. Their aim is honourable and in the main well intentioned, they want to help show conclusively that there is an existence and a rich, fulfilling universe waiting for us; that death is NOT the end. Assurance that this is the case would undoubtedly provide a tangible degree of comfort to many people who grieve for a loved one or, indeed, fear their own demise.

However, sadly, unless they continually monitor their methods even these groups will eventually be drawn into the highly stylised, overly-dramatic, self-serving and synthetic world of those whose aims in this field are rather less than altruistic. There are of course highly respected and long established organisations like the Society for Psychical Research (SPR) and its Scottish equivalent the SSPR. The findings of these august bodies are generally considered as very 'safe' and guarded, but to be fair it is easy to see why, because there are many detractors who delight and relish dismissing and debunking anything that smacks of the paranormal or supernatural. The same set of negative reactions applies to parallel (and similarly named) serious investigative organisations existing in other countries.

The high profile groups I refer to are those who set themselves up as rather flashy arbiters of how and when to contact traces of the dead, because the means they use are, in many cases, dubious and often laughable. There are several culprits and all, perhaps inadvertently, complicit in what they do, but two of the worst offenders comprise one which unfailingly uses the 'technical approach' like The Atlantic Paranormal Society (TAPS) promoted by the Syfy (sic) Channel. The other non-technical approach is used by those involved with the long running British TV series, Most Haunted (MH).

MH normally went out on Living TV on one of the satellite channels, although it is now seen on the free-to-air digital service. It has been claimed by one of the original mediums on MH that its remarkable success saved Living TV from financial disaster. Before continuing it's worth making the point that these shows, and others like them, appear on TV heralded as for 'entertainment only', because they cannot be used as proof of an afterlife, the broadcasting regulations forbid it. This is not the case with religious programmes however, which promote the existence of an equally paranormal all powerful entity, i.e. Almighty God, on the basis of considerably less evidence. It is an inconvenient truth that all religions bar none are based solidly on what amounts to paranormal phenomena by any other name.

The Methods

TAPS tends to arrive at their target locations armed with flight cases loaded with electronic measuring equipment of various kinds, e.g. oscilloscopes, frequency counters, EMF meters, digital thermometers, video cameras, sound recorders, TV cameras and monitors etc, etc. There is no good reason for this because there is absolutely no consensus on what the phenomena is, never mind how it functions. Presumably the extravagant use of such hi-tec equipment somehow legitimises what they do and of course looks very impressive on-camera to a largely credulous and uncritical audience. In fact, in some ways the use of various types of measuring and recording equipment and the situation that creates resonates with the warning about mediums taking payment for their services. While no one would quibble about the need to earn a living, when mediums charge for their services then an expectation is automatically created, because if someone pays for a service they are entitled to expect results. Similarly for the medium, if they take a fee then there is pressure to produce a result; any result, which may, and in the past has, led to both misrepresentation and outright fraud.

The fact is that impressive as all the equipment looks, in many cases those using it have neither a clear understanding of what the equipment measures nor, crucially, what the readings indicate. By this I mean is an anomaly in the electromagnetic field created by the phenomenon, or does the phenomenon create the anomaly? Why are drops in temperature sometimes assumed to be a sign of a paranormal event? There are no easy answers to these questions; assertions and speculation in abundance, but no real answers. In the case of the non-technical approach used by the MH team; this consists of minimal use of electromagnetic field (EMF) meters to establish 'base line' readings, and anything that is measured that deviates from this may or may not indicate the presence of something anomalous.

This of course chimes neatly with the baseless assumption that apparitions operate in same part of the spectrum monitored or measured by the device. It has been said that as far as human beings are concerned and how we interact with the electromagnetic universe, if the EM universe was as long as the Mississippi river, the portion that the human race can interact with unaided would be around one inch long. Using instrumentation we can and do monitor and use other portions of this spectrum from the infra red to the ultraviolet, but our equipment good though it is can only go so far, so we have no understanding of what might exist beyond these ranges and that goes in particular for amateur investigative groups whose equipment has to be both affordable and commercially available. It might be informative to learn what ranges are accessible to the kind of equipment available to the military, or perhaps research laboratories. Yes, some amateur groups can and do design their own equipment, but this kind of project is very few and far between and is also hampered by the underlying fact that once again, and I repeat: *there is absolutely no consensus on where to look or what to look for.*

As far as the TV shows mentioned here are concerned, a guest medium or sometimes more than one, is introduced (and the MH show has had several), who will then walk through whatever area is selected, hopefully making contact with the 'departed'. Another issue with programmes of this kind is that they are *expected* to produce results, so are any 'revelations' that might ensue necessarily valid? Irrespective of the method used, almost everything with the possible exception of electronic voice phenomena (EVP), is based entirely on the subjective opinions of the medium or other sensitive. The EVP's are *assumed* to be voice impressions left by the spirits of the dead captured or various types of recording device (including tape machines and digital recorders of various sorts) in response to questions asked by the investigators.

The Ovilus

Again, this is all well and good, but (especially with the 'technical teams') these alleged 'responses' to questions are passed through various kinds of software, including frequency analysers and filters to extract what may or may not be a message. These messages are often extracted from what seems to be no more than blips in the background hiss created by the automatic gain circuits that many of these recorders use. Automatic gain serves as handy adjunct to a manual sensitivity control on voice recorders, which would normally require to be adjusted by hand to compensate for various levels of background noise. To make matters worse, as is normally the case on the TV shows the viewer is then helpfully prompted by a line of scrolling text which allows them to decipher what is being said, otherwise the 'message' is an absolutely meaningless distortion open to any interpretation.

While what follows is by no means an endorsement for one particular device, one modern incarnation and there are many, of equipment currently used in conjunction with EVP experiments is called the 'Ovilus', which is available in a range of types and in its latest incarnation features a voice synthesiser plus a digital display simultaneously showing the word (or words) being spoken by the supposed 'spirit entity'. This is a very good idea, because by the nature of what it is, in some cases what the artificial voice says is not easy to understand. It is not like the relatively 'human' voice heard on 'sat-navs', this voice is wholly synthetic and it sounds like it too.

To be fair, given the notoriously litigious nature of the law in the United States the manufacturer is wise enough not to make specific claims about what the Ovilus does; they market it (shades of the broadcasting regulations) with a series of declaimers purely as an 'entertainment device'. The unit operates in a range of modes and converts several environmental factors, (e.g. EM fields of various kinds plus temperatures), into numerical values and applies them to a stored library of words and phrases, although in some cases (based on the model) it can form non-stored words based on other parameters. This of course assumes that 'spirit' is able to manipulate the ambient EM field and access the stored library to convey what it is trying to communicate in the first place. The trouble is that in most cases the responses from the Ovilus appear to be entirely spurious and random and bear little if any obvious relationship to the questions asked. This tends to lead the user to try framing their questions to suit the answers rather than the other way round, which rather defeats the purpose of the exercise.

I should add that this does mean that units like this do not permit genuine communication, but it does make some pretty pointed assumptions about the nature of what we as human beings are trying to communicate with. Not least that the entities have an instinctive understanding of complex electronics and how they function and are able to make them usable on their terms in order to communicate. Perhaps if they are energy based they share common parameters so they can and do, or perhaps they can operate electronic equipment at the atomic level, who knows? But, again, this is entirely speculative. Yes, unfortunately many organisations persist in using these highly dubious methods, but there is one group that does not and that is GSI Paranormal, which was created by Don Phillips. What is also notable about GSI is that unlike many other groups purporting to investigate paranormal phenomena, it treats the spirit world and those who dwell there with the respect they deserve.

Don, GSI and Becky

There are a number of vital differences that set this group apart from the rest, one is the relationship that Don has developed with his spirit guides, or his 'friends' as he calls them and in this case it is a better description: although perhaps 'colleagues' might be an even better term since this is effectively a working relationship. I say this because the entire subject of the paranormal, especially the fairly rarefied aspect of spirit communication, which as we have seen is weighed down heavily with outdated, unwanted and unneeded Victorian baggage. At any rate Don co-operates with his friends/colleagues, a female spirit called, (or calling itself) 'Becky' is one of the regulars, to make contact with others who have made the final transition.

The other major factor is that Don does not need elaborate equipment to make the communications audible or decipherable. The replies to his questions, which are captured on straightforward digital recorders, in this case high-end Olympus devices, are sometimes easily decipherable straight from the recording device without the need for any filtering, help or prompting; they really can be that clear. I do emphasis the words 'can be' here, because often they are not, or at least not to me. Another remarkable factor about the type of work done by Don and his group is his 100% success rate in moving on (effectively exorcising) unwanted and frequently malignant entities and that is quite a record. These demonstrations of EVP's coupled with the successful 'exorcisms' have attracted a fair number of detractors both from his competitors and of course from the establishment of 'experts', all of whom are only too pleased to dismiss what he is doing as nothing more than well-meaning smoke and mirrors at best, and at worst outright fraud.

Fortunately, he is able to provide abundant first class evidence for his claims and the proof of the pudding is always in the eating, or listening in this case. If things proceed as they have and the evidence continues to grow apace, it is only a question of time before what he is demonstrating on a daily basis will prove, finally and conclusively, that we can and do move on to a non-physical state of existence after death. What's more, life after life has many parallels with what we experience now, inasmuch as we continue to develop, evolve and mix with others who have already made the transition. The truly poignant and wonderful thing is that, to reprise what I said earlier about comfort, our loved ones can still make contact with us here in the physical realm. It seems as if eternity is much more than just an abstract concept and Don Phillips just might be able to supply a reliable means of contact.

'Becky'

So, a little more about 'Becky': I have to make clear that what follows is taken in good faith more or less verbatim from communications Don has had with this female spirit Becky. I either accept this or I do not, and in the absence of anything to the contrary I have chosen to do so. Apparently her full name is Becky Michaels and according to Don she died as the result of a plane (or train) crash in 1995. She has been in semi-permanent contact with him almost since he created GSI and as a result a remarkably close and trusting relationship has developed between them. According to what Becky has told him she actually lives in his house and is sometimes frustrated that he cannot see her. Becky, who was born in Leister Royal Infirmary, was married and had two children, Michael and Emily, who were killed in the same accident.

She was cremated after her death, but it is not clear what happened to her children, Don says that this information is not forthcoming and neither is the location of the cemetery where her ashes are located. Becky has also told him that their meeting was preordained and that she is destined to help and also protect him, this seems to mean that he is 'defended' from the predations of demonic entities. The demonic entities that appear surprisingly often seem to have a curious relationship with him as well and have repeatedly asked him to join them because this would make him 'more powerful', (whatever that means) and they have also offered to make him rich. Of course Becky is not the only spirit who communicates with him, but she is the most regular. One more thing about Becky is that because her parents are still alive, (but as she says 'very old') both she and Don requested a degree of circumspection about what is reported: it is also why he has not told them about their daughter.

I met Don as a result of an email that arrived out-of-the-blue in my inbox. The email pretty much stated what he could do and I answered it in a fairly brief manner saying that these were pretty big claims. I did this on the basis that at the time I was the editor of Paranormal Magazine and received many such claims and to be honest this was no more or less convincing than several others. Don replied with several examples backing up what he said and things developed from there and we have since spoken at length many times and find that we share similar views on a range of subjects relating to the paranormal.

As a result of the conversations, a wide range of related topics have been discussed, including the nature of what lies on the other side of physical death, the reason that Don is able to talk to the other side with relative ease, plus a host of other related topics. The conversations have also included some what might be construed as words of caution for me, where I have suggested that he might be getting 'used' by some of these beings for their own ends. Don is sure that he is not and his relationship with most of these entities is mutually beneficial. I have little choice other than either abandon our friendship or take Don at his word, which is what I have chosen to do, although always tempered with caution. Other aspects of our lengthy conversations have included questions regarding the comparative simplicity of the way in which he talks to the disembodied intelligences, until I finally asked a question that piqued both of our interest: it is the question that is the *raison d'etre* for this chapter, viz: *'Was there a spirit world before the Big Bang?'* The answer to this (received via Becky) was, to say the least, extremely perplexing and enigmatic.

Fighting the War in Heaven

The first response was that *'There was a lot of fighting'* and no further information was forthcoming at that time, it was a reply that provided considerably more questions than answers. In the course of pursing this strand of enquiry Don received what could be construed as a veiled threat concerning group of beings who may (or equally may not) be called the 'Lightertons', or perhaps that should be 'Litertons'. I should emphasise that there is absolutely no consensus on how this word is spelled or if it is even relevant, but this group, or their representatives, made it clear via the communications that this is what they are called, they were aware of him and the implication was that he should leave questions like that well alone.

One might ask why? Why should asking questions about the nature of Heaven or the beginning of time be of consequence to anyone other than the person asking them? Why would these 'Litertons' (in the absence of anything to the contrary we'll settle for that spelling) want any questions or enquiries suppressed? I should point out that since this was the first time Don had heard the word he was not sure if it was the name of a family who had lived in the area at one point or something else. He checked local records, but could find no sign of anyone with the unusual family name 'Literton' (or 'Lighterton') and assorted variants, so he had to enquire further afield.

The comments about 'A lot of fighting' struck me as somehow relevant, but nothing came to mind until a few days later. Out of nowhere came a line from The Book of Revelation 12:7, *'There was a war in Heaven'*. The quote as referenced in 1984 The New International version reads: *'And there was war in Heaven. Michael and his angels fought against the dragon and the dragon and his angels fought back',* there are other translations of this in other versions of the Bible, but all say more or less the same thing. The quotation refers to the way in which Satan (and by association Hell) came into being when God cast him and his rebellious fellow angels out of Heaven for refusing to accept that human beings had immortal souls and as such put them, partly at least, on a similar footing of the angelic host.

For the record I should make crystal clear that as far as the Bible and its contents are concerned I am extremely ambivalent and in most cases tend to dismiss it as a mixture of allegory, folk tales, myths, legends and fiction. Nevertheless it may still contain a few nuggets of fact that have been altered to suit the understanding and culture of those who wrote it. Perhaps it also contains what we might refer to as 'race memories' that have been programmed into our DNA and continue to find expression in ancient traditions. Rather disconcertingly it has been calculated that millions of Christians, especially in America, accept scripture as the literal truth.

This is doubly worrying when one considers that the Quran is also seen as the literal and revealed word of God/Allah (the same thing) and that Muslims regard it in exactly the same way and any criticisms or dissent are regarded as valid reasons to kill those making them. At any rate, the relevance of Becky's statement about 'fighting' and 'The War in Heaven' might be linked, but there is no real way of saying whether or not this might have occurred before the Big Bang or after it. What it did do, however, was give some kind of link which, if true, might attach credibility to what is said in the bible and the beginning of the universe and all it contains. What it does not do however is legitimise religion, but that is not the purpose of this chapter.

Shortly after making the connection between Becky's comments and the scriptural war in Heaven, I contacted Don and told him what I thought and his response was strange yet heartening. Evidently when Becky wants to let him know that she is either present or has an opinion on something she conveys this by transmitting what he calls an 'energy rush' and he can feel this. Using the term, 'energy rush' is hardly scientific nor is it specific, but unfortunately such is the frequently ephemeral nature of the phenomenon and since there is no accepted common denominator then it is as good a definition as any. When I told Don about my thoughts he experienced an immediate and powerful 'rush' from Becky. He took this to mean that she approved of it, or at least had no objections, because if she had there would either have been a 'negative feeling' (and yes, I am fully aware that is entirely subjective), or no response at all.

As a result of the questions I asked, Don spent a considerable time talking to Becky and the answers he received revealed much that seemed to resonate with other ancient tales that have their roots in scripture and elsewhere. It also makes for some extremely interesting comparisons regarding the nature of what we consider as 'Heaven', because it appears as if Heaven may well be an alternate universe incredibly close to our own, but due to the way in which it functions is unreachable in a physical form. This vexed question about the fighting; what did that actually mean? Fighting where, with whom and for what? What was the outcome and what happened to the losers in this conflict. This was certainly squaring up with everything we have ever been taught about angels and demons, Heaven and Hell.

What are angels and were they ever human? According to Becky, depending on their role, angels are awarded 'power' (yet another infuriatingly loose and indefinable term) and ability as they need it. The use of the word 'role'; once again this is slightly nebulous because according to tradition there are various groupings of angels called 'choirs' ranging from sort of utilitarian 'entry model' angels, right on to the immensely powerful 'seraphim' whose power is almost limitless, but they are of course all ultimately answerable to God. All the major religions recognise the existence of angels as mediators and go-betweens acting as filters between the human race and God, but what they are and where they actually came from (do they also predate the Big Bang?) is open to question.

Another extremely curious statement was the very nature of the parallel universe. This, according to Becky was intended for 'Heavens people', what did that mean? Who are 'Heavens people'? Are they the angels or something else entirely? Are 'Heavens people' guarded by these angels? Can they communicate with them; can we communicate with them? Were the losers in this Heavenly battle inherently evil? Were they templates for all that is evil, did they in effect become demons? It's probably a good idea here to say that what New Age teaching perceives as angels are almost certainly not the same as the angels of scripture and have more in common with either benevolent ET's (or possibly fairies, another New Age favourite) than anything spiritual.

However, one question in particular produced one of the most surprising responses. Don asked if God existed and what came back by way of reply was remarkable and in some ways extremely unsettling. The normally single voice became a multitude, almost a choir shouting out, *'We adore him, we adore him'*. This response, aside from the obvious, may imply a whole lot of things, one being the old saying attributed to Satan that, *'My name is legion for we are many'*. While it may well be that these spirits with whom Don communicates are what they say they are, once again comes the worrying possibility that equally they are not, and this is something we have to consider. Again this unease about ancient warnings in John 8:44 about the 'Prince of Lies', i.e. *'When he lies, he speaks his native language, for he is a liar and the father of lies.* In other words he/it/they will do anything necessary to get what he/it/they want, and I do mean *anything*. Don and I have discussed this matter at length many times, but despite my own reservations about it (and I still have them), Don seems happy to continue on the route he has taken, relying on the entities he has befriended to keep him safe from harm.

Becky and The Litertons

We have already encountered the race of beings, if that is what they are, that call themselves 'Litertons' and once again they quite unexpectedly made contact with Don some time later during one of the frequent conversations he has with his group of spirit colleagues. Once again during a brief lull in the conversation he picked up a short sentence on his recorder announcing that the Litertons were there, but, as is their nature, they were either unwilling or unable to provide much more information other than to say that 'something' unspecified was going to happen. Don got the impression that this 'something', whatever it was, was somehow UFO related. Since the information came from this unlikely source it tends to lend credence to the view that aside from mistakes on the part of the witnesses, natural events and military 'black projects', what are seen in the skies around this planet may be overt manifestations of what we currently define as the paranormal.

This time however Don specifically asked Becky about the Litertons and received the unambiguous response that they were *'very ancient'*, but once again there was an apparent reticence to talk about them. This caused Don to decide that he should make a determined effort to get in contact with them again and if they were willing conduct a detailed conversation with them. We should keep in mind that whatever these beings are they are under no obligation whatsoever to respond to a request for contact and even if they did, that any answers that might be forthcoming would be either relevant or even truthful. That said if they are, as Becky says, 'very ancient', many fascinating insights into the nature of the human race and the invisible worlds that surround us might be forthcoming. Becky also gave a little bit more information about this group of beings, although in fact what she had to say does not exactly clarify the situation.

What she said was this; the Litertons are mostly 'good' spirits that have, 'never been human'; they originate on another planet, are 'much closer than you think' and live 'mostly in water'. Unfortunately, from Don's point of view he is unable to establish contact with them (the Litertons) as often as he would like, because as we have seen they only communicate as and when they feel inclined to do so. However, shortly after this another apparently completely contradictory message concerning the Litertons arrived from Becky saying that, *'We have to stop them'*. Don obviously wanted to know more, and typical of the major frustrations attached to anything involving the 'other side', he could not get any further response to his questions. As always it is very much a work in progress, one thing he did note was then when they communicate their messages are powerful and much clearer than those from other spirits.

This creates another problem, especially when the comment that the Litertons, 'have never been human' comes into the equation. 'Never been human' can mean a number of things and feeds back into the discussions I have had with Don on numerous occasions regarding the nature of these entities and indeed of Becky herself. Apart for the obvious, i.e. that they are by their very nature literally non-human, there is another and much more worrying interpretation, that they are in fact demons. Demons likewise have never been human, but continually seek the means by which to gain access to the physical realm and unfortunately this can mean taking possession of a human host.

The other thing to consider is that they are patient very, very patient, and will wait indefinitely until they get their chance. However, for once Don in the absence of anything else is inclined to accept the possibility that they very well might be demons, but of some higher rank, assuming that demons have a hierarchical structure. I should emphasise that while this book was being written Don had a series of encounters with demons, or entities claiming to be demons, because there is a difference, in his own home. What follows comes verbatim from an email Don sent to me describing this particular encounter.

Don's Email

It's 2am in he morning, my wife and I were about to settle down to some well earned sleep after a very busy day, lights out. Five minutes later I felt a very strong presence. It didn't feel like my guy's (Don describes his spirit helpers as 'my guys') so I grabbed the recorder off the bedside cabinet, because I even take them to bed with me. I asked 'Who's that'? A very loud demonic sounding voice instantly replied "We're after you", or "We've come for you", or words to that effect. I then said "Who the Hell do you think you are turning up here in my home with your threats? I then said "Ok, cut the crap, show me what you got, let's do this now". It/ they replied "I'll wait till your dead!

I replied "You know you can't touch me and if you wait till I'm a spirit at least we will be on a level and I'll still beat you". The following night in the early hours of the morning whilst in my workshop (I should explain that Don, a former IT technician, regularly communicates with his 'team' from a workshop that is part of his house), it/they again appeared, this time by request, they said, "You know we're going to take you", but after a few exchanges they left.

The last time there was such a strong negative entity was in my room the phone rang between two and three am, it was a friend, David (pseudonym).He was suicidal saying he was going to end it all there and then and just wanted to say thank you before they did. My friend was in a very upset state and crying down the phone, I said, "Don't do a thing, don't say a word, just wait a minute". I then picked up the recorder and without saying a word just hit the record button, before I played it back a very loud whispery voice came out of the air above my bed, my wife and I both heard it say, "We're going to kill David".

My wife was extremely nervous and when I played the recorder back the voice [that had first come from mid air came from the speaker on the recorder saying the same thing. I then said to David who was still on the phone, and fortunately he had not heard this exchange, "There may well be a reason you're feeling this way" and told him what my wife and I had just experienced. This had an immediate effect and within two minutes of speaking to him he was in a more positive state of mind. A few days later a much more relaxed David visited me and I played them the recording. "You're fucking kidding me" was the response on hearing it.

I do not advise anyone under normal circumstances to either engage or challenge negative entities, but for reasons that I am unable to go into at this time for me this does not present a problem. I have had spirits around me since around the age of seven and I'm now forty seven years old. In that time I have learned much about both them as well as myself. People often underestimate what they cannot see and base their perceptions of such entities on what they have read somewhere and this is often incorrect. Negative entities are far more capable than many people give them credit for and often extremely subtle in choosing their targets and how they attack (the people are usually already in a delicate state of mind).

This short exchange describes exactly why I have warned Don repeatedly about his relationship with these entities; I still have many reservations. However that aside, from what Becky has said it does seem to chime with at least one of the more avant-garde interpretations of the entities that inhabit the realms normally ascribed to spirit and if not demonic then what? It is a definition that crosses, blurs and blends the accepted boundaries between ghosts, spirits and, infuriatingly, Ufology, or more importantly the beings assumed by convention to be non-terrestrials who are part and parcel of this phenomenon.

However, if what Becky says gives another glimpse into the real nature of the 'spirit world', then once again it seems as if the conventional view of the paranormal is in dire need of re-interpretation. What this also does is give further impetus and credibility to the investigative work carried out by the previously mentioned Scole Group in the late 1990's when they tried to obtain proof of the continuation of consciousness after physical death. As already mentioned as part of that series of experiments they obtained an image of an entity they called 'Blue'.

That was not its given name (it had none), but instead described what they captured on the 35mm colour film stock they used, the image had a blue tinge, I should point out that this was before the widespread use of digital photography. What was ever more interesting was that it was identical to the 'grey' aliens who are part and parcel of UFO mythology. The Scole group were informed that it (and indeed other strange beings) inhabited a parallel reality existing alongside our own. Again if that is the case then the subject of UFO's, ET's and the nature of spirit may be even more interlinked and stranger than we think. It also may reinforce the possibility that these Litertons, and in fact demons and angels as well, may have some other basis in reality, but rather than anything spiritual, they could well actually be existing in another dimension that, if the Scole Group (and of course some of the more exotic branches quantum physics) are right, is one of many.

Authors Note

This chapter was indirectly inspired by a short story from the pen of the remarkable and iconic early 20th century American author Howard Phillips (HP) Lovecraft. The tale, 'Dreams in the Witch House', involved a troublesome and particularly malicious witch, Keziah Mason, who in 1692 was imprisoned in a Salem jail and before coming to trial managed to escape her cell by simply walking right through one of the walls. She did this by using blood to draw a geometric diagram (possibly a sigil, this is not made clear in the story) of some kind on the wall, which somehow altered physical reality and created a portal through which she passed into regions unknown. In effect this is a description of inter-dimensional travel, which is theme common to much of Lovecraft's work, in fact it is possible to define most of his literary output as science fiction rather than genre horror.

This always struck me as somehow appropriate and seemed to reflect the implications of some areas explored by quantum physics that hint at something similar. This is especially true when one considers that perhaps some of the equations developed by physicists have more than a passing similarity to the sigils use by magicians, after all if we can understand the nature of reality might we be able to alter it? In case you are unfamiliar with the term, sigils are complete spells or incantations that, by removing certain letters and words then recombining what is left, have been reduced to their very essence, condensed if you like, into images and patterns of immense power.

I have also deliberately, but unavoidably, used various terms like 'sprit', 'ghost', 'poltergeist' and 'séance' to describe various events and the energies that cause them to occur. In the context of what follows I do not think these terms have any particular relevance and may actually be detrimental because they carry much unwanted and unneeded baggage. However, in the short term and for want of something more suitable, I decided to use them simply because most people have become accustomed to them and by and large know what they imply. As more is discovered and understood about the phenomenon a new and more accurate vocabulary may have to be devised to reflect these discoveries.

Chapter 13
The Poltergeist Equations

"Future science will consider quantum mechanics as the phenomenology of particular kinds of [an] organised complex system, quantum entanglement would be one manifestation of such organisation, paranormal phenomena another. As yet, our understanding of such matters is very qualitative, but application of the skills of the physicist to such situations can be expected to yield more precise theories in due course."

Prof Brian Josephson, (1940 -)

The above astute observation made by Professor Brian Josephson, the former head of the *'Mind–Matter Unification Project in the Theory of Condensed Matter'*, at the Cavendish Laboratory at Cambridge University in the UK makes a clear connection between particle physics and the paranormal. Another physicist who makes a similar connection, this time between particle physics and mystical experience, especially eastern spirituality, is Fritjof Capra whose book, 'The Tao of Physics', makes this very clear. Yet another physicist, David Bohm, when he comments about the possible holographic nature of the universe and by extension consciousness, adds his two-pence worth and seems to agree with Prof Josephson and as a result we have ended up with the curious notion of 'quantum mysticism'.

This, when taken in the context of what was also said by one of the founders of transpersonal psychology, the psychiatrist Prof Stanislav Grof, viz, *'If one makes an honest assessment of quantum physics, consciousness research, Oriental spiritual philosophies and shamanism, one cannot help but come to the conclusion that consciousness can modify phenomena in the material world'*, just about sums up the current state of play. In fact the more one looks at the nature of the human condition, especially as it relates to consciousness, it becomes clear that we are inextricably connected to what we both can and cannot see in just about every way imaginable. If that is the case, then perhaps quantum mysticism is an appropriate description of what we are dealing with, i.e. magick (yes, the spelling is deliberate, it is designed to separate a genuine phenomenon from trickery and illusion) redefined for a modern era.

On the other hand, in the interests of fairness it has to be said that Prof David Deutch, an equally eminent theoretical physicist who, along with Richard Feynman and others, helped create the basis for quantum computation, dismisses it as nothing more than a mixture of delusion and wishful thinking. This is doubly strange, because the very properties that allow a quantum computer to operate, i.e. 'superposition', or the theoretical ability for a particle to exist in more than one state at any given moment (e.g. to simultaneously be both on and off or in any state in between) is the very thing that inspired the other physicists who have taken the opposite view.

I should add that there is no shortage of equally qualified physicists who share the view of Prop Deutch. Therefore let me make it clear that what follows is open to debate and based on what might best be called 'informed speculation', because, other than the obvious physical manifestations of what we currently define as 'poltergeist phenomena', there is absolutely no consensus on what the poltergeist phenomenon is or, in particular, the mechanism by which it functions. Yes, there is plenty of guesswork and unfortunately much of it is contradictory, but absolutely nothing set in stone so it is a subject where various theories have equal validity.

In this instance I have chosen to examine some of the possibilities suggested by recent discoveries made in the still hotly disputed area of quantum physics. This is, as we have seen, an absolutely legitimate area of science where, because the rules that govern it are so different from the norm, much of what has been found seems to defy much older (and perhaps safer) scientific principles based on solid Newtonian physics. As a result the implications are frequently disputed even by the scientists who work in this discipline. Even Sir Isaac Newton, the iconic polymath and genius upon whose pioneering and visionary work much of modern science is based, felt instinctively that there was a driving force, something fundamental and unseen behind the discoveries he made and memorably observed that, *'The universe is a cryptogram set by the almighty'*. Sir Isaac could see that what he discovered was based on something infinitely more profound; it was a puzzle that he spent his entire life trying to solve. It is highly significant that during the era in which Newton lived he was sometimes regarded as both a heretic and a magician.

In other words, science of all sorts often reveals truths that have earth shattering implications and quantum science is a highly specialised field where what was traditionally regarded as impossible, magickal even, might just have some basis in reality. What must also be kept in mind is that where anything connected, however loosely, to the paranormal is concerned, apart from those who habitually think 'outside the box' anyway, scientists of whatever hue tend to have an inherent mistrust of what they cannot readily quantify or measure. Therefore, even for the majority of those involved in the truly bizarre and frequently mind-bending world of particle physics, the existence of disembodied or discarnate intelligence is still a step too far… and this is despite what some aspects of their theories and equations imply.

The Poltergeists
With that in mind; the utterly bizarre nature of poltergeists and what they are capable of has bedevilled humanity for almost as long as the existence of disembodied intelligence has been

suspected. Sometimes the actions of these frequently unruly entities seem totally pointless and random with no obvious rhyme or reason, mindless in fact to the point of being created not by intelligence, but by something purely arbitrary, physical and equally unknown. On some occasions what occurs seems to be malicious and deliberately harmful and it is possible that in these instances whatever is causing the effects may not be a spirit in the accepted sense at all. In times past when cases such as this occurred, there was a distinct overlap between what was considered as demonic interference and more prosaic ghostly manifestations. Given the often violent and abrupt nature of poltergeist activity is not hard to see why the association was made, especially in those relatively naive and superstitious times. While ghosts were feared at least there was a level of acceptance and they could be tolerated, but anything deemed demonic was seen as downright harmful and absolutely rejected.

Whether or not the poltergeist phenomenon is some random, unknown natural process or caused by a discarnate intelligence does not detract from the fact that there is a mechanism being used that can, in some manner, act as an interface to channel a form of energy and interact directly with the physical world. In mundane terms 'work' is being done, therefore energy is being expended and that has to some from somewhere, there are no 'free lunches', ever. On one level, since 'cold spots' are often recorded during encounters with spirit it may be that the energy comes from there, thermal energy converted into kinetic (or sometimes acoustic) energy. It's basic thermodynamics and the conservation of energy is being maintained, but this does not explain other phenomena because the range of what can occur is vast. This includes objects moving and vanishing, but can also involve writing, direct speech, smells and even communication via telephones both land line and mobile, including, incredibly, text messages.

However, although the phenomena can sometimes appear malicious, at other times what occurs is relatively benign (although often capricious), and in both manifestations there frequently seems to be a measure of intelligence and control involved where the entity can and does respond to questions and reacts to requests. Rather than try to give an explanation for all of these occurrences, because even the laws of thermodynamics do not explain all of it, it might be easier to concentrate on one of the strangest of the alleged poltergeist abilities, which is the way these entities, or something acting on their behalf, causes items to spontaneously materialise and dematerialise. By doing so we might also shed some light on how the other manifestations occur. The materialisation and de-materialisation of objects has close parallels with the phenomenon of 'apports', the name given to items that are alleged to occasionally (and spontaneously) appear in séance rooms.

Apports

Because they share many of the properties common to poltergeist materialisations let's pause for moment to consider these apports. In a purely spiritualist setting the term 'apport' is given to any object that appears spontaneously in the course of a séance. Normally, each apport should have specific meaning to one or more of those present at the séance and they are intended to demonstrate the reality of contact with the afterlife in a tangible manner. The objects are normally small, e.g. brooches, pebbles or buttons (although there are reports of fresh flowers and fruit appearing), but irrespective of what the objects may be, like the items materialised by poltergeists they manifest instantaneously in the séance room and appear to travel through solid matter to get there.

In some instances they fall with a thud upon the floor or table, in others they appear to drift down as if virtually weightless then gain weight quite quickly. In many cases they are warm to the touch (temperatures of 40 degrees Centigrade have been recorded), certainly much warmer than the normal ambient temperature of the séance room. If this phenomenon occurred in isolation it would be reasonable to assume it was solely an adjunct of spiritualist phenomena, but it does not, it has parallels right across the entire paranormal/UFO spectrum. Since the objects are warm to the touch, one way in which this might happen is if they were dismantled right down to their component atoms and then reassembled; how else could they pass through walls? Either that or the frequency or 'phase' of their structure was altered to something other that that of the walls through which they pass, because if they were the same they could not pass through, something that may resonate with the way in which poltergeists de (and re) materialise objects

The Quantum Factor

One of the really odd aspects that single out the dematerialisations and re-materialisations produced by poltergeists is that they never occur *whilst the objects are being observed* (my emphasis) and that is vital. It is always when there is no one actually looking at them. In a matter of seconds, and sometimes literally only in the time it takes to blink an eye during which sliver of time the object is not observed, it has vanished so where has it gone? It flicks out of our reality only to reappear elsewhere, usually nearby and sometimes in a drawer or other sealed container, or, as we have seen, perhaps a séance room. Not only has in reappeared, but in the manner of the previously mentioned 'apports' it has also passed through solid matter to do so, why, how does this happen?

Why does the object not vanish (or reappear) when it is actually being watched, why must the human element in this equation not actually be the in act of observing the object, even if only peripherally? Does this do more than hint at the nature of the realm inhabited by the entities we refer to as phantoms, ghosts, poltergeists or any of the other traditional terms we use to describe them? As we shall see, is it possible that they are 'probability waves' or even 'potentials' existing at the edges of reality and does this imply that they need human beings to permit their existence? Because if it does it is another link between the quantum world and what happens there and the world of spirit; the same argument has been used in respect of the ghosts, if there were no human beings there would be no ghosts and for exactly the same reasons: they _need_ human beings to exist.

None of this is by any means straightforward and we must first consider two ideas drawn from quantum physics; one is called '*the many worlds theory*' and the other, which we touched on earlier, is '*quantum superposition*' to which it is closely allied. The first theory states that the universe and everything in it exist as a series of probability waves that only become realities when decisions are made about them. This seems to imply that unless the world, and indeed the universe around us, is not constantly watched it would not exist. However, even that rather worrying notion was modified by another theoretical physicist, the late Hugh Everett. Without getting too technical because the implications are truly mind numbing, every bit as much as poltergeist phenomena itself, what it boils down to is this and I apologise in advance for what follows, but in order to make my point I have little choice so please bear with me.

According to Everett, the wave functions that comprise reality do not collapse, but shoot off as variants on all possible outcomes of the original; this phenomenon is what lies at the heart of quantum computing, mentioned at the beginning of this article. In other words the universe and everything in it exist in this strange state and you more or less create reality from nanosecond to nanosecond by either observing or making a decision about it. I suppose this is a riff on the old Buddhist thought puzzle about 'if a tree falls in the forest and there is no one there to hear it, does it make sound? The second of these propositions, 'quantum superposition', has as we have seen, powerful and almost magical resonances with this and holds that physical objects like electrons, or atoms for that matter, exist simultaneously in all possible states, but when measured (or in our case are observed) give a result corresponding to only one such state.

This is also born out by the famous 'double slit' experiment, which seems to indicate that subatomic particles are somehow aware that they are being observed or monitored and behave accordingly. In the double slit experiment the particles, in this case photons, acted like particles 93% of the time they were observed and like waves when they were not. This may imply that our thoughts do have a very real effect at the vanishingly small level of particle physics and if that is the case then perhaps willpower does work externally of the mind. What this also does is give some credence to ancient animistic beliefs, i.e. that every single thing in creation has a measure of intelligence (or was animated, hence 'animist'), they instinctively understood this, but not why; and to be fair for all our sophistication we still don't.

Before continuing further it is important to understand one thing, because it is all too easy to become hopelessly bogged down in theory; the equations of quantum physics do not describe actual existence; they predict the potential for existence and this parallels the doctrine of Mahayana Buddhism. Part of the philosophical canon of Mahayana Buddhism is 'Sunyata', which usually translates into English as 'emptiness', but in the original Sanskrit it also contains elements of 'potential'; something that is considered in the aforementioned book, 'The Tao of Physics'. However at the harder edge of science it is also true that no discrepancy has ever been found between the equations of quantum theory and experimental observations made using these calculations.

What this infers is that there is interaction between particles irrespective of the distance between them through 'quantum entanglement', or that everything in the universe is entangled with everything else at the subatomic level; it is a condition that also appears to defy both time and space. However, the 'opposite particle' is empty of its own existence until it is defined by the presence of mind. In other words they exist in the 'other universe' only as potentials and do not become real until a mind interacts with the potential and alters its state to one of 'reality', in short as the previously mentioned Stanislav Grof implies, if there is no mind there is no reality. Once again this conclusion chimes with teachings on Sunyata and although the evidence is staring us in the face, conventional science sticks grimly to its formulae and measurements, dismissing the claims of psychics and mystics as fantasy and nonsense. Perhaps they need the comfort and certainly that their discipline brings.

Bizarrely, even while adopting this inflexible stance, they press ever further into the unseen quantum universe and are now developing a method to image the 'ghost twin' of any particle, in this case photons. They propose to do this by using 'Quantum Holography', which should create a three dimensional image of the entangled particle by measuring the interference created by its possible paths. While the science of quantum holography is still theoretical, researchers claim that there are no technical reasons why such a detection system could not be built. It is difficult to see why they are so entrenched in their views when the very experiments they conduct clearly suggest that all is far from what it seems to be.

So, what has this to do with the materialisation and otherwise of objects when you are not actually looking at them and yes, I know we are on the shakiest of ground here? By not actually looking at the object you are denying, or no longer legitimising, its place in reality and perhaps the entity, assuming it exists on the same plane, is able to interact with the object because they are both in the same state of existence (or non existence) from our physical perspective. Again is seems to suggest that for this to work the poltergeist would have to exist at the same potential as the probability wave and they are a kind of 'uncertainty potential' just waiting for the chance to use their utterly unique vantage point to interact with physical reality, because the object once not seen loses its ability to remain 'real' in our sense of the word.

While that might go some way to explaining why objects do not vanish while being observed, i.e. by looking at them you are fixing or establishing their position, it does not explain the method by which the poltergeist is able to interact with the physical world and actually move the object, unless this occurs while the object is in it's dematerialised atomic state of potential. It is almost as if the odd effects seen to occur at the quantum level are somehow being magnified and are occurring at the physical level. Again we are faced with qualifying words like 'as if', 'appear' and 'seem', but we have no choice here, because we are dealing in a world of possibilities, probabilities and intangibles.
If the spirit entity can actually acquire an object in its non-observed potential state and draw it into its own version of reality, then they both exist at the same potential and crucially both retain their individuality. This would also happen in our reality when we handle or interact with an object, so they would have exactly the same relationship with the object as we would with something existing in our reality. If they move the object and place it elsewhere it is then still in a state of potential existence until we actually see it and, like Schrödinger's famous dead/alive cat, it springs back into being again

This is the stuff of magick and what we have seen is that at one level the possibility of magick is very real indeed and that the equations developed by physicists describe the processes going on around us and by doing so define them. Rather like the witch in the Lovecraft tale that opened this article, what physicists are actually doing is creating a new generation of magick spells and incantations, spells that reach into the realms beyond physical reality and describe what lies there hidden from human view, but perhaps available to whatever entities are already there. This was broadly hinted at when the Scole Experiment was under way and the possibility emerged that we are surrounded by multiple layers of reality inhabited by a variety of entities. What we have seen is that somehow materialisations and dematerialisations take place and while there is no solid explanation why, it has to be a factor of the electromagnetic quantum universe in which we live and now we understand that while the answers still may not be obvious, what we can do now is offer at least one feasible answer.

Afterword

'Battle not with monsters lest ye become a monster and if you gaze into the abyss, the abyss gazes also into you',
Friedrich Nietzsche (1844 - 1900)

The word, 'Heretic', so often associated with spiritual rebellion and even sorcery, literally means the much less alarming, *'One who chooses'*. This book, which is derived from many different yet inescapably interlinked sources, is intended to allow you, the seeker into occult and magickal lore, to peer through the cracks in the façade of normality that has been constructed to conceal many dark and frequently uneasy truths concerning the human condition. Doing so deserves some timely words of warning and caution and you should consider your position very carefully. As the quotation by Nietzsche states, *'if you gaze into the abyss, the abyss gazes also into you'*, and indeed it does as many who chose the rocky path to truth and enlightenment discovered.

At one stage in the history of our race your instinctive curiosity would have automatically condemned you as a heretic and your route to official 'salvation', (if it was even offered), would have been short, brutal and, more likely than not, agonising. It is curious to learn that salvation and forgiveness frequently equated with death and your path to a hypothetical pardon was often glimpsed through the flames engulfing you at the stake. While there are currently no official proscriptions denying the natural instinct of curiosity, you should keep firmly in mind that history is cyclical, and because of this humanity, in spite of all its abundant talent, is almost guaranteed through inherent stupidity, pride and intolerance to repeat its mistakes. This also includes those who claim to be 'liberal' and 'inclusive' because there are many varieties of liberalism that are every bit as intolerant, harsh and dictatorial as the oppressive ideologies they claim to replace.

Among the first things your quest will unearth are the unmistakable links between magick, the occult and religion and in spite of continuous repudiations and denials by the religious authorities we find that these subjects tread similar paths and in the past have even worn the same shoes. All religions from the very earliest times were founded on a 'revelation' in one form or another made to an individual and this revelation frequently came from what was considered to be an 'angel' or some other supernatural agency. Is it likely that these wondrous entities had no religious provenance whatsoever, and both they and their agendas may have originated in some murky and far off, invisible *'otherworld'*?

Could this entity have been one of the beings also allegedly unleashed in recent times by such relatively modern magicians as the notorious Aleister Crowley, Jack Parsons and L. Ron Hubbard the inventor of Scientology; and indeed, are they still among us? The inclusion of Hubbard in the same company as known magicians may seem unlikely, but this individual was, along with Jack Parsons and to some extent the notorious Crowley, responsible for *'The Babalon Working'*, which was a ritual intended to open a portal in the fabric of reality to allow an alien entity, in this case the goddess Babalon, access to this planet. In fact Hubbard has much in common with a series of unlikely messiahs who either began as magicians or had that title bestowed upon them.

In bygone eras for example is it not strange that the prophet Mohammed encountered an 'angel', Gabriel, from who he learned the precepts of Islam, or many centuries later that Joseph Smith, the founder of Mormonism, had a very similar encounter with an 'angelic' being called Moroni? In both cases the precious metal, gold, was involved, Gabriel presented Mohammed with a 'golden tablet' commanding him to read it and Moroni gave Joseph Smith 'magical spectacles' called *'Urim and Thummim'*, with which to translate texts written in an unknown language called 'reformed Egyptian', these texts were oddly enough, also written on 'golden plates'. Why specifically gold?

Was this because its intrinsic value implied great wealth and therefore lent the story greater significance, or might it simply have been a factor of the electrical properties of the metal? Does this hint at the possibility that properties inherent in magick and the occult may be a factor of the electromagnetic spectrum? An even earlier instance of initiation comes from the Gnostic mystery school of *'Manichaeism'*. In this case, at the age of twelve the founder, Mani, encountered a being that he referred to as *'The Twin'*. This being imparted a great secret, which revealed that evil had continually influenced the human race and that there was a continual battle throughout the cosmos between the opposing forces of good and evil.

This mystery school was quite widespread and even counted St Augustine among its many initiates. Another apparent connection between the early church and magick involves Bishop Clement of Alexandria, who taught his advanced students what he called the *'disciplina arcani'* (lit. secret disciplines), which were, in effect, magickal practises and techniques. This supposed cosmic battle finds a strange resonance in claims from sections within the UFO community suggesting that there is a battle currently raging in the cosmos concerning the takeover of planet Earth and its inhabitants. In this scenario a race known as *'The Nordics',* (who seem to conform to the western angelic stereotype being attractive, tall, blue-eyed blondes), are on the side of humanity, while enemy have all the characteristics of demons etc. typified by images of greys and reptilians.

The reader will find a few more synchronous crossovers between magick, religion and Ufology as they progress through this afterword, is this by accident or design, or does the era, culture and context define reality? Magick and magickal beliefs in the form of animism and latterly shamanism existed long before religion and, in spite of religion's best efforts to stifle them they have continued to exist in parallel with it and will, in spite of everything, continue to exist; one must ask oneself why? One must also ask why considerable sums of money have been spent by various government agencies all over the world attempting to harness 'magickal' forces for their own purposes; the infamous and previously mentioned Stargate Project was case in point. Is this possible, is this practical, or is it something that only exists in the tales of wizardry created by writers of fantasy fiction?

Perhaps writers like H.P. Lovecraft may even have succeeded in breaching the gateways, reaching into bizarre and unnameable worlds that exist beside our own, although in the case of Lovecraft the creatures he describes appear to have been glimpsed in some inter-dimensional version of Hell. In other words, as with many instances involving the occult, the only difference between fantasy and reality lies in the perspective and cosmology of the observer. Might the horrors the writers envision actually exist in some altered reality and gradually drip-feed into their subconscious minds to find a type of specious existence in the written word? Or more worryingly, might the very act of reading about them in some way alter the neural processes in the brain of the reader and present them with the chance to materialise in our world? Is their malign influence the real driving force behind the actions of the serial killers and multiple rapists who prey on our largely passive society? Or are the tales simply words of warning about dimensional entities whose potential for hatred and malice is unknowable?

Other heretical utterances concern the presence of the human race here on Earth. How did we get here and could our moon have provided the means to do so, or was there another method? We find bizarre experiments conducted in 1953 by Millar and Urey to recreate the building blocks of life and even claims that a strange form of life was created, apparently artificially, during the curious Crosse experiment in the mid 19th century. Was Darwin right or did he fail to grasp a much bigger picture simply because the concept required was too vast, conservative religious values to deeply entrenched and the prevailing science was just not up to proving it?

The instinctive and repressive influence of religion tried to stifle his breakthroughs and to some extent still does, indeed Creationism casts a long, long shadow and still flourishes in the American 'bible belt'. But what happens now that geneticists operating at the current leading edge of science announce the creation of the first genuinely artificial biological life form? Dr Craig Venter and his team in the USA have taken the first step and created a single cell that is synthetic. A single cell may seem like small beer, but this is only the beginning and its eventual benefits are alleged to include the creation of custom made human organs for donation and this is well and good, but what happens when the first entirely synthetic human is finally created; what then? A miracle, magick or science and is there necessarily any difference: the ethical and moral implications and considerations are enormous; might this even be a step too far.

When you continually 'push the envelope' might the envelope finally tear and if it does what lies on the outside? While not a heresy in a conventional sense, does the fact that we *can* do something mean that we actually *should* do it and are there some areas of research best left alone? Is this moral and ethical minefield an example of the abyss that stares right back into us? Never forget that conservative religion always tried to deny anything that did not fit its self serving and cosy canon of belief even when its dogmas are proven utterly wrong. However, science has had a profound effect on religion, but religion has had little or no effect on science, except as we saw earlier, to occasionally use it as source of heresy with which to condemn it.

Has our race evolved as far as it can or is the future already here, just waiting in the wings until the conditions are right for it to emerge? One thing linking all of these seemingly disparate issues are the subjects that opened this book, the pale, inseparable spectres of magick and religion, but they now seem to find expression in a number of much more subtle and diverse guises. There is however hope, for although what is suggested here may not exactly induce peace of mind, it just might create a need for greater understanding of what is real and what is not and what has value and what does not, and in that search for knowledge the seeker might find the source of their own salvation. Since to some extent we select our own road in life and the vehicle in which to travel, we should choose both wisely.

Sources and references for all chapters

Part One
The Paranormal and Ufology

The Occult, Superscience and The Third Reich
The Invisible Eagle by Alan Baker pub Virgin, ISBN 1-85227-863-3
The Hunt for Zero Point by Nick Cook pub Arrow, ISBN 0-09-941498-8
The UFO Hunters Handbook by Bret Leuder pub Watkins Publishing, ISBN 978-1-78028-543-6
naziconspiracy.onlc.eu/14-The-Freiburg-UFO-crash-of-1936-the - 17k
www.crystalinks.com/haunebunaziuofs1936.html - 13k -
fairfieldproject.wikidot.com/karotechia
occultthirdreich.wordpress.com/category/karotechia/
en.wikipedia.org/wiki/Ahnenerbe
www.carnwyffa.u-net.com/documents/karotechia.html
www.bibliotecapleyades.net/sociopolitica/reichblacksun/...
english.pravda.ru/society/anomal/14-01-2013/123470-thir...
ovni.do.sapo.pt/principal/antartica/antarct_ingl/VRIL3ingl.h - 11k
en.wikipedia.org/wiki/Die_Glocke - 85k –
www.zamandayolculuk.com/cetinbal/htmldosya1/NaziUFO5.htm - 74k -
en.wikipedia.org/wiki/Vril - 54k –
www.militaryfactory.com/aircraft/detail.asp?aircraft_id=105
www.unexplained-mysteries.com/forum/index.php%3Fshowtop...
www.dummies.com/how-to/content/alien-secrets-the-vril-societ - 48k -
www.bibliotecapleyades.net/esp_sociopol_vril.htm - 26k -
www.bibliotecapleyades.net/sociopolitica/sociopol_vril07.htm - 51k
www.schauberger.co.uk/ - 5k
en.wikipedia.org/wiki/Viktor_Schauberger - 63k
jnaudin.free.fr/html/repulsin.htm - 11k –
discaircraft.greyfalcon.us/Viktor Schauberger.htm - 33k
en.wikipedia.org/wiki/Flying_saucer

https://en.wikipedia.org/wiki/Northrop_YB-35
en.wikipedia.org/wiki/German_nuclear_energy_project –
thevelvetrocket.com/2009/08/25/the-nazi-nuclear-program-how-clo...
discaircraft.greyfalcon.us/JFM.htm
www.godlikeproductions.com/forum1/message1028387/pg1
en.wikipedia.org/wiki/Frank_J._Tipler –
naziufomythos.greyfalcon.us/majorlusar.html
www.unrealaircraft.com/wings/german_discs.php
magonia.haaan.com/2009/nazi-ufo-02/ - 62k
sites.google.com/site/nazibelluncovered/
www.bbc.co.uk/news/world-middle-east-22629920
en.wikipedia.org/wiki/Ernest_Rutherford
www.nytimes.com/2013/05/23/world/middleeast/irans-nucle...
bipartisanpolicy.org/sites/default/files/Iran%2520Nucle...
en.wikipedia.org/wiki/North_Korea_and_weapons_of_mass_d...
en.wikipedia.org/wiki/Norwegian_heavy_water_sabotage
www.damninteresting.com/heavy-water-and-the-norwegians/
www.theatlantic.com/international/archive/2013/04/how-n
www.tldm.org/News9/PossessionHitlerStalin.htm
msgboard.snopes.com/message/ultimatebb.php%3F/ubb/get_t...
paranormal.about.com/od/hollowearth/a/aa022206_2.htm
www.agoracosmopolitan.com/home/Frontpage/2008/07/14/024

Truth, Lies and Ufology: Disinformation and Paul Bennewitz
www.serpo.org/article3.php
www.greatdreams.com/Falcon-Richard-Doty.htm
www.sandia.gov/locations/albuquerque_new_mexico/visiting_alb
en.wikipedia.org/wiki/Sandia_National_Laboratories –
www.godlikeproductions.com/forum1/message1367419/pg1
www.tbp.org/pages/publications/Bent/Features/F99Poteat.pdf
www.topsecretwriters.com/2011/02/project-palladium-had-cuban
.wikipedia.org/wiki/Dulce_Base
en.wikipedia.org/wiki/UFO_conspiracy_theory
www.exopolitics.org/dulce-report.html
projectcamelot.org/bennewitz.html
www.bibliotecapleyades.net/bb/bennewitz.htm -
www.osi.andrews.af.mil/ - 40k –
oregonmufon.com/PDFs/UFODisinformation.pdf –
brumac.8k.com/kirtland1.html
en.wikipedia.org/wiki/Newspeak
www.ufocasebook.com/robertsonpanel.html
www.roswellproof.com/dyvad1951.html -
www.foia.cia.gov/ufo.asp
www.cufos.org/IUR_article3.html - 38k -
en.wikipedia.org/wiki/Psychological_Strategy_Board

en.wikipedia.org/wiki/Bay_of_Pigs_Invasion
www.jstor.org/stable/10.2307/40107707
www.projectbluebook.us/page-5.htm -
www.blackvault.com/documents/ufos/c_a/robertson0.htm
www.think-aboutit.com/ufo/project_aquarius.htm
www.projectaquarius.net/ -
www.excludedmiddle.com/Moore interview.html
en.wikipedia.org/wiki/Bill_Moore_(ufologist)
en.wikipedia.org/wiki/Majestic_12 - 187k
vault.fbi.gov/Majestic 12 –
www.ufocasebook.com/documents.htm_
cyraxandflyrax.wordpress.com/2011/10/30/dulce-alien-undergro
www.cosmicchannelings.com/blog/k_nightmare-hall

Dark Days at Plum Island: Government Research, Hybrids and Technology.
www.ibconsultancy.eu/cbrne/explosives/history-of-explos...
en.wikipedia.org/wiki/Chemical_warfare
en.wikipedia.org/wiki/Porton_Down
hmg.oxfordjournals.org/content/8/9/1631.full
www-cs-faculty.stanford.edu/~eroberts/courses/ww2/proje...
www.emedicinehealth.com/biological_warfare/article_em.h.
www.whale.to/a/in_the_grip_of_mad_scientists.html
www.britannica.com/EBchecked/topic/938340/biological-we...
en.wikipedia.org/wiki/Biological_warfare
en.wikipedia.org/wiki/Ricin
en.wikipedia.org/wiki/Poisoning_of_Alexander_Litvinenko -
dvice.com/archives/2010/06/future-soldiers.php
www.dailymail.co.uk/sciencetech/article-2017818/Embryos...
news.nationalgeographic.co.uk/news/2005/01/0125_050125_...
www.bbc.co.uk/wiltshire/moonraking/spooky_ufo.shtml
www.sptimes.com/News/102801/Worldandnation/Island_with_...
www.adventurebound.com/blog/13-of-the-worlds-most-infam...
www.openculture.com/2012/09/watch_student_science_exper...
en.wikipedia.org/wiki/International_Space_Station
www.forteantimes.com/features/articles/1302/lost_in_spa...
beforeitsnews.com/space/2013/01/ufo-sightings-at-intern...
en.wikipedia.org/wiki/Unit_731
www.deepblacklies.co.uk/unit731-part1.htm
en.wikipedia.org/wiki/Chimera_(genetics)
www.scq.ubc.ca/the-truth-about-chimeras/
propaganda-dimitrios.blogspot.com/2011/07/uk-scientists...
http://www.christianpost.com/news/british-scientists-create-animal-human-hybrids-52802/#sGS3xHPQjuzm1q3c.99
https://sites.google.com/site/mcrais/voices

www.cufon.org/cufon/malmstrom/malm1.htm
www.ufohastings.com/articles/ufos-reported-near-malmstr...
en.wikipedia.org/wiki/Sarin_gas_attack_on_the_Tokyo_sub...
www.bio.net/bionet/mm/neur-sci/2000-January/042872.html
www.bibliotecapleyades.net/ciencia/ciencia_psychotronic...
en.wikipedia.org/wiki/ECHELON
en.wikipedia.org/wiki/PRISM_(surveillance_program)
www.experian.co.uk/business-strategies/mosaic-uk.html
www.mosaicsoftware.co.uk/knowledge-centre/glossary.aspx
https://en.wikipedia.org/wiki/Government_Communications...
news.bbc.co.uk/2/hi/503224.stm
en.wikipedia.org/wiki/Greenham_Common_Women%27s_Peace_C...
www.bibliotecapleyades.net/scalar_tech/esp_scalarweapon

Dissonance and the True Believer.
en.wikipedia.org/wiki/End_time
www.nowtheendbegins.com/
https://en.wikipedia.org/wiki/UFO_religion
en.wikipedia.org/wiki/List_of_UFO_religions
michaelsheiser.com/UFOReligions/
en.wikipedia.org/wiki/Cognitive_dissonance
web.mst.edu/~psyworld/cognitive_dissonance.htm
www.sevenraystoday.com/secretoftheandes.htm
hiddenlighthouse.wordpress.com/tag/brotherhood-of-the-s
www.freewebs.com/awordfitlyspoken/isaacnewton.pdf
www.standard.co.uk/news/the-world-will-end-in-2060-acco...
en.wikipedia.org/wiki/Isaac_Newton%27s_religious_views
www.truthmagazine.com/archives/volume7/TM007017.htm
www.catholic.com/quickquestions/what-is-the-significance-of-the...

The ET Inside
en.wikipedia.org/wiki/Darwinism
www.urbandictionary.com/define.php?term=Abiogenisis
cience.howstuffworks.com/science-vs-myth/everyday-myth...
en.wikipedia.org/wiki/Anthropic_principle
en.wikipedia.org/wiki/Late_Heavy_Bombardment
profiles.nlm.nih.gov/ps/access/SCBCCP.pdf
en.wikipedia.org/wiki/Directed_panspermia
en.wikipedia.org/wiki/Charles_Darwin
en.wikipedia.org/wiki/Miller%E2%80%93Urey_experim...
www.truthinscience.org.uk/tis2/index.php/component/cont...
creation.com/why-the-miller-urey-research-argues-agains...
www.biology-online.org/biology-forum/about17447.html
en.wikipedia.org/wiki/Spontaneous_generation

Hiding in Plain Sight?
'Alien Dawn' by Colin Wilson pub 1999 Virgin ISBN 0-7535-0395-6
'UFO's: Operation Trojan Horse' by John A. Keel pub 1971 ABACUS
en.wikipedia.org/wiki/Our_Lady_of_F%C3%A1tima
en.wikipedia.org/wiki/Our_Lady_of_F%C3%A1tima
en.wikipedia.org/wiki/User:Zacherystaylor/The_Fatima_UFO_Hypoth...
www.mt.net/~watcher/bvmsandufos.html
www.angelfire.com/journal/imagearchives/Lourdes/archivedirectory.html
www.phantomsandmonsters.com/2012/02/fatima-ufo-hypothesis.html
'Alien Agenda' by Jim Marrs pub 1997 Harper ISBN 0-06-109686-5
'UFO's and the PSI Interface' various authors, pub 2001 BUFORA
'Fortean Times' Issue 222 pub May 2007

The Extraterrestrial Hypothesis and the Periodic Table: Is the final answer to the ET question here?
en.wikipedia.org/wiki/Lockheed_A-12 –
en.wikipedia.org/wiki/Foo_Fighters
www.project1947.com/articles/arwwr.htm -
www.ufoevidence.org/cases/case482.htm
www.ufoevidence.org/cases/case880.htm
en.wikipedia.org/wiki/Gulf_Breeze_UFO_incident
en.wikipedia.org/wiki/Phoenix_Lights –
en.wikipedia.org/wiki/Dulce_Base
beforeitsnews.com/blogging-citizen-journalism/2013/03/dulce-und
www.greatdreams.com/Falcon-Richard-Doty.htm
www.webelements.com/
www.chemicalelements.com/ -
The Things that Nobody Knows: William Hartson, pub 2012 by Atlantic Books ISBN 9780 8578 9622 3

Part Two
Everyday Magick

Christ, The Shroud and The Rainbow Body
'The Hidden Science of Lost Civilisations' by David Wilcock, publisher Souvenir Press ISBN 1-455-8284-7-5
'The Field' by Lynne McTaggart, publisher Harper Collins   ISBN 0-06-093117-5
'The Physical Phenomena of Mysticism' by Herbert Thurston publisher Roman Catholic Books ISBN 13: 9781929291515
'A Brief Guide to Ghost Hunting' by Dr Leo Ruickbie, publisher Robinson, ISBN 978-1-78033-826-2
en.wikipedia.org/wiki/Veil_of_Veronica
www.christisnotrisen.com/shroud.html

www.shroud.com/bar.htm
en.wikipedia.org/wiki/Rainbow_body
ayangrinpoche.org/an-introduction-to-phowa. www.khandro.net/
mustardseed_phowa1.htm
www.fractal.org/Life-Science-Technology/Peter-Gariaev.htm
www.emergentmind.org/gariaev06.htmen.wikipedia.org/wiki/Fritz-
Albert_Poppwww.wddty.com/human-energy-fields-fritz-albert
popp.htmlwww.elcollie.com/st/light.htmlshop.hauntedcuriosities.com/GLOWING-
PHENOMENON-95

Rock 'n' Magick:The Strange Connections Between Rock Music, the Occult and Advertising
'Your Thoughts Are Not Your Own': by Neil Saunders, publisher NumberSixDance
Publishing UK ISBN N/A
cremationofcare.com/the_nwo_subliminal_abuse.htm
en.wikipedia.org/wiki/Solfeggio_frequencies
solfeggiofrequencies.net/
www.miraclesandinspiration.com/solfeggiofrequencies.htm.
www.forteantimes.com/features/articles/94/the_devils_ch...
www.geneveith.com/2011/07/27/the-devils-interval/
www.guardian.co.uk/notesandqueries/query/0,,-1767,00.ht..
backwardmessages.wordpress.com/2011/06/30/death-metal-o..
www.forteantimes.com/features/articles/91/the_rosslyn_c...
www.illuminati-news.com/art-and-mc/occult-rock.htm
en.wikipedia.org/wiki/The_Exorcist_(film)
www.helpfreetheearth.com/news103_Disney.html
en.wikipedia.org/wiki/Gruen_transfe
http://www.mycultlife.com/tag/cult-jacob-aranza/
http://en.wikipedia.org/wiki/Backmasking

Get Thee Behind Me Satan!: Demonic Possession and Exorcism
en.wikipedia.org/wiki/Nicole_Aubrey
carlomac.net/angels/Laon.html
en.wikipedia.org/wiki/Urbain_Grandier
en.wikipedia.org/wiki/Loudun_possessions
www.williamhkennedy.com/witchcraft.html
www.hutchisoneffect.ca/
www.damninteresting.com/the-hutchison-effect/
rationalwiki.org/wiki/John_Hutchiso
www.skepdic.com/hutchisonhoax.html

Slayers: The Last Vampire Hunters
en.wikipedia.org/wiki/Antinous
www.antinopolis.org/ -
rationalwiki.org/wiki/Se%C3%A1n_Manchester

en.wikipedia.org/wiki/Highgate_Vampire
friendsofbishopseanmanchester.blogspot.com/
redpill.dailygrail.com/wiki/Sean_Manchester
rationalwiki.org/wiki/David_Farrant
www.holygrail-church.fsnet.co.uk/FarrantFacts.htm
en.wikipedia.org/wiki/Highgate_Vampire
www.gothicpress.freeserve.co.uk/The%20Highgate%20Vampire.htm
mysteriousuniverse.org/2013/05/revisiting-the-highgate-vampire/
en.wikipedia.org/wiki/Montague_Summers
www.gothicpress.freeserve.co.uk/Montague%20Summers.htm
www.luxmentis.com/blog/?p=981
en.wikipedia.org/wiki/Old_Catholic_Church
www.oldcatholicchurchuk.com/
www.oldromancatholic.org.uk/
en.wikipedia.org/wiki/Aleister_Crowley
strangeattractor.co.uk/further/glasgows-metal-toothed-vampire-panic/
en.wikipedia.org/wiki/Southern_Necropolis –
en.wiktionary.org/wiki/right_of_sepulchre
www.definitions.net/definition/right+of+sepulchre
www.historic-scotland.gov.uk/human-remains.pdf

Before The Beginning

en.wikipedia.org/wiki/Big_Bang
science.howstuffworks.com/dictionary/astronomy-terms/before-big...
www.bbc.com/future/story/20130502-what-came-before-the-big-bang
en.wikipedia.org/wiki/Many-worlds_interpretation
www.dummies.com/how-to/content/the-theory-of-parallel-universes...
www.happy-science.org/the-truth-of-the-spirit-world -
en.wikipedia.org/wiki/Spirit_world_(Spiritualism)

The Poltergeist Equations

en.wikipedia.org/wiki/Many-worlds_interpretation
listverse.com/.../10-mind-bending-implications-of-the-many-worl... –
en.wikipedia.org/wiki/Category:Quantum_mysticism
www.triumphpro.com/isaac-newton-and-end-time-prophecies-of-daniel.pdf
en.wikipedia.org/wiki/Stanislav_Grof –
en.wikipedia.org/wiki/Quantum_superposition –
www.tcm.phy.cam.ac.uk/~bdj10/ -
en.wikipedia.org/wiki/Quantum_computer -
www.markvernon.com/.../dotclear/index.php?.../Quantum-mysticism
search.informit.com.au/fullText;dn=318897024107124;res=IELHSS
esoterx.tumblr.com/.../the-holographic-universe-and-the-paranor...
www.beliefnet.com/Faiths/.../What-Mahayana-Buddhists-Believe.as...
www.patheos.com/Library/Mahayana-Buddhism.html
en.wikipedia.org/wiki/Conservation_of_energy

www.thescoleexperiment.com/
www.afterlife101.com/Scole_1.html
www.hplovecraft.com/writings/fiction/dwh.aspx
www.dagonbytes.com/thelibrary/lovecraft/dreamswitchhouse.htm -
https://www.goodreads.com/.../13278166-the-dreams-in-the-witch-house

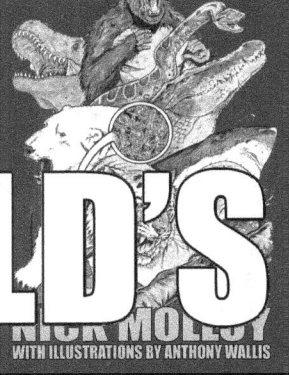

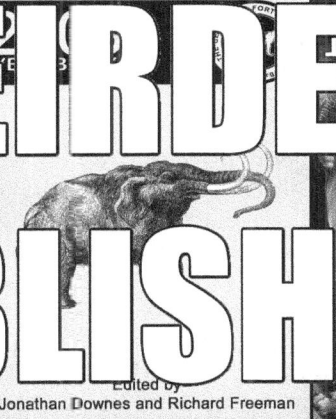

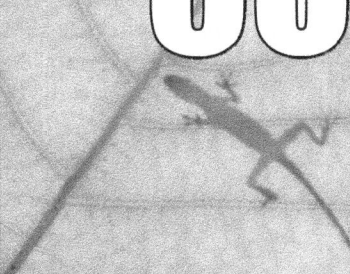

HOW TO START A PUBLISHING EMPIRE

Unlike most mainstream publishers, we have a non-commercial remit, and our mission statement claims that "we publish books because they deserve to be published, not because we think that we can make money out of them". Our motto is the Latin Tag *Pro bona causa facimus* (we do it for good reason), a slogan taken from a children's book *The Case of the Silver Egg* by the late Desmond Skirrow.

WIKIPEDIA: "The first book published was in 1988. *Take this Brother may it Serve you Well* was a guide to Beatles bootlegs by Jonathan Downes. It sold quite well, but was hampered by very poor production values, being photocopied, and held together by a plastic clip binder. In 1988 A5 clip binders were hard to get hold of, so the publishers took A4 binders and cut them in half with a hacksaw. It now reaches surprisingly high prices second hand.

The production quality improved slightly over the years, and after 1999 all the books produced were ringbound with laminated colour covers. In 2004, however, they signed an agreement with Lightning Source, and all books are now produced perfect bound, with full colour covers."

Until 2010 all our books, the majority of which are/were on the subject of mystery animals and allied disciplines, were published by `CFZ Press`, the publishing arm of the Centre for Fortean Zoology (CFZ), and we urged our readers and followers to draw a discreet veil over the books that we published that were completely off topic to the CFZ.

However, in 2010 we decided that enough was enough and launched a second imprint, `Fortean Words` which aims to cover a wide range of non animal-related esoteric subjects. Other imprints will be launched as and when we feel like it, however the basic ethos of the company remains the same: Our job is to publish books and magazines that we feel are worth publishing, whether or not they are going to sell. Money is, after all - as my dear old Mama once told me - a rather vulgar subject, and she would be rolling in her grave if she thought that her eldest son was somehow in `trade`.

Luckily, so far our tastes have turned out not to be that rarified after all, and we have sold far more books than anyone ever thought that we would, so there is a moral in there somewhere...

Jon Downes,
Woolsery, North Devon
July 2010

Other Books in Print

Wildman! by Redfern, Nick
Globsters by Newton, Michael
Cats of Magic, Mythology and Mystery Shuker, by Karl P. N
Those Amazing Newfoundland Dogs by Bondeson, Jan
The Mystery Animals of Pennsylvania by Gable, Andrew
Sea Serpent Carcasses - Scotland from the Stronsa Monster to Loch Ness by Glen Vaudrey
The CFZ Yearbook 2012 edited by Jonathan and Corinna Downes
ORANG PENDEK: Sumatra's Forgotten Ape by Richard Freeman
THE MYSTERY ANIMALS OF THE BRITISH ISLES: London by Neil Arnold
CFZ EXPEDITION REPORT: India 2010 by Richard Freeman *et al*
The Cryptid Creatures of Florida by Scott Marlow
Dead of Night by Lee Walker
The Mystery Animals of the British Isles: The Northern Isles by Glen Vaudrey
THE MYSTERY ANIMALS OF THE BRITISH ISLES: Gloucestershire and Worcestershire by Paul Williams
When Bigfoot Attacks by Michael Newton
Weird Waters – The Mystery Animals of Scandinavia: Lake and Sea Monsters by Lars Thomas
The Inhumanoids by Barton Nunnelly
Monstrum! A Wizard's Tale by Tony "Doc" Shiels
CFZ Yearbook 2011 edited by Jonathan Downes
Karl Shuker's Alien Zoo by Shuker, Dr Karl P.N
Tetrapod Zoology Book One by Naish, Dr Darren
The Mystery Animals of Ireland by Gary Cunningham and Ronan Coghlan
Monsters of Texas by Gerhard, Ken
The Great Yokai Encyclopaedia by Freeman, Richard
NEW HORIZONS: Animals & Men issues 16-20 Collected Editions Vol. 4 by Downes, Jonathan
A Daintree Diary -
Tales from Travels to the Daintree Rainforest in tropical north Queensland, Australia by Portman, Carl
Strangely Strange but Oddly Normal by Roberts, Andy

Centre for Fortean Zoology Yearbook 2010 by Downes, Jonathan
Predator Deathmatch by Molloy, Nick
Star Steeds and other Dreams by Shuker, Karl
CHINA: A Yellow Peril? by Muirhead, Richard
Mystery Animals of the British Isles: The Western Isles by Vaudrey, Glen
Giant Snakes - Unravelling the coils of mystery by Newton, Michael
Mystery Animals of the British Isles: Kent by Arnold, Neil
Centre for Fortean Zoology Yearbook 2009 by Downes, Jonathan
CFZ EXPEDITION REPORT: Russia 2008 by Richard Freeman *et al*, Shuker, Karl (fwd)
Dinosaurs and other Prehistoric Animals on Stamps - A Worldwide catalogue
by Shuker, Karl P. N
Dr Shuker's Casebook by Shuker, Karl P.N
The Island of Paradise - chupacabra UFO crash retrievals,
and accelerated evolution on the island of Puerto Rico by Downes, Jonathan
The Mystery Animals of the British Isles: Northumberland and Tyneside by Hallowell, Michael J
Centre for Fortean Zoology Yearbook 1997 by Downes, Jonathan (Ed)
Centre for Fortean Zoology Yearbook 2002 by Downes, Jonathan (Ed)
Centre for Fortean Zoology Yearbook 2000/1 by Downes, Jonathan (Ed)
Centre for Fortean Zoology Yearbook 1998 by Downes, Jonathan (Ed)
Centre for Fortean Zoology Yearbook 2003 by Downes, Jonathan (Ed)
In the wake of Bernard Heuvelmans by Woodley, Michael A
CFZ EXPEDITION REPORT: Guyana 2007 by Richard Freeman *et al*, Shuker, Karl (fwd)
Centre for Fortean Zoology Yearbook 1999 by Downes, Jonathan (Ed)
Big Cats in Britain Yearbook 2008 by Fraser, Mark (Ed)
Centre for Fortean Zoology Yearbook 1996 by Downes, Jonathan (Ed)
THE CALL OF THE WILD - Animals & Men issues 11-15
Collected Editions Vol. 3 by Downes, Jonathan (ed)
Ethna's Journal by Downes, C N
Centre for Fortean Zoology Yearbook 2008 by Downes, J (Ed)
DARK DORSET -Calendar Custome by Newland, Robert J
Extraordinary Animals Revisited by Shuker, Karl
MAN-MONKEY - In Search of the British Bigfoot by Redfern, Nick
Dark Dorset Tales of Mystery, Wonder and Terror by Newland, Robert J and Mark North
Big Cats Loose in Britain by Matthews, Marcus
MONSTER! - The A-Z of Zooform Phenomena by Arnold, Neil
The Centre for Fortean Zoology 2004 Yearbook by Downes, Jonathan (Ed)
The Centre for Fortean Zoology 2007 Yearbook by Downes, Jonathan (Ed)
CAT FLAPS! Northern Mystery Cats by Roberts, Andy
Big Cats in Britain Yearbook 2007 by Fraser, Mark (Ed)
BIG BIRD! - Modern sightings of Flying Monsters by Gerhard, Ken
THE NUMBER OF THE BEAST - Animals & Men issues 6-10
Collected Editions Vol. 1 by Downes, Jonathan (Ed)
IN THE BEGINNING - Animals & Men issues 1-5 Collected Editions Vol. 1 by Downes, Jonathan
STRENGTH THROUGH KOI - They saved Hitler's Koi and other stories

by Downes, Jonathan
The Smaller Mystery Carnivores of the Westcountry by Downes, Jonathan
CFZ EXPEDITION REPORT: Gambia 2006 by Richard Freeman *et al*, Shuker, Karl (fwd)
The Owlman and Others by Jonathan Downes
The Blackdown Mystery by Downes, Jonathan
Big Cats in Britain Yearbook 2006 by Fraser, Mark (Ed)
Fragrant Harbours - Distant Rivers by Downes, John T
Only Fools and Goatsuckers by Downes, Jonathan
Monster of the Mere by Jonathan Downes
Dragons:More than a Myth by Freeman, Richard Alan
Granfer's Bible Stories by Downes, John Tweddell
Monster Hunter by Downes, Jonathan

TRADE MARK
BEWARE OF IMITATIONS
CFZ CLASSICS

CFZ Classics is a new venture for us. There are many seminal works that are either unavailable today, or not available with the production values which we would like to see. So, following the old adage that if you want to get something done do it yourself, this is exactly what we have done.

Desiderius Erasmus Roterodamus (b. October 18th 1466, d. July 2nd 1536) said: "When I have a little money, I buy books; and if I have any left, I buy food and clothes," and we are much the same. Only, we are in the lucky position of being able to share our books with the wider world. CFZ Classics is a conduit through which we cannot just re-issue titles which we feel still have much to offer the cryptozoological and Fortean research communities of the 21st Century, but we are adding footnotes, supplementary essays, and other material where we deem it appropriate.

Headhunters of The Amazon by Fritz W Up de Graff (1902)

Fortean Words

The Centre for Fortean Zoology has for several years led the field in Fortean publishing. CFZ Press is the only publishing company specialising in books on monsters and mystery animals. CFZ Press has published more books on this subject than any other company in history and has attracted such well known authors as Andy Roberts, Nick Redfern, Michael Newton, Dr Karl Shuker, Neil Arnold, Dr Darren Naish, Jon Downes, Ken Gerhard and Richard Freeman.

Now CFZ Press are launching a new imprint. Fortean Words is a new line of books dealing with Fortean subjects other than cryptozoology, which is - after all - the subject the CFZ are best known for. Fortean Words is being launched with a spectacular multi-volume series called *Haunted Skies* which covers British UFO sightings between 1940 and 2010. Former policeman John Hanson and his long-suffering partner Dawn Holloway have compiled a peerless library of sighting reports, many that have not been made public before.

Other books include a look at the Berwyn Mountains UFO case by renowned Fortean Andy Roberts and a series of forthcoming books by transatlantic researcher Nick Redfern. CFZ Press are dedicated to maintaining the fine quality of their works with Fortean Words. New authors tackling new subjects will always be encouraged, and we hope that our books will continue to be as ground-breaking and popular as ever.

Haunted Skies Volume One 1940-1959 by John Hanson and Dawn Holloway
Haunted Skies Volume Two 1960-1965 by John Hanson and Dawn Holloway
Haunted Skies Volume Three 1965-1967 by John Hanson and Dawn Holloway
Haunted Skies Volume Four 1968-1971 by John Hanson and Dawn Holloway
Haunted Skies Volume Five 1972-1974 by John Hanson and Dawn Holloway
Haunted Skies Volume Six 1975-1977 by John Hanson and Dawn Holloway
Grave Concerns by Kai Roberts

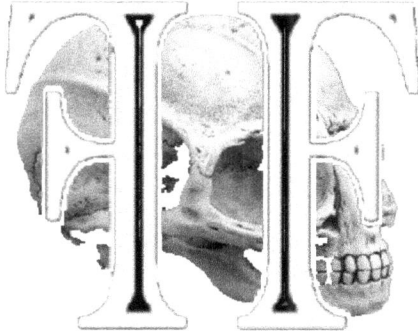

Fortean Fiction

Just before Christmas 2011, we launched our third imprint, this time dedicated to - let's see if you guessed it from the title - fictional books with a Fortean or cryptozoological theme. We have published a few fictional books in the past, but now think that because of our rising reputation as publishers of quality Forteana, that a dedicated fiction imprint was the order of the day.

We launched with four titles:

Green Unpleasant Land by Richard Freeman
Left Behind by Harriet Wadham
Dark Ness by Tabitca Cope
Snap! By Steven Bredice
Death on Dartmoor by Di Francis
Dark Wear by Tabitca Cope
Hyakymonogatari Book 1 by Richard Freeman

www.ingramcontent.com/pod-product-compliance
Lightning Source LLC
Chambersburg PA
CBHW070838300326

41935CB00038B/1135